MARK NOBLE

Boleyn Boy

MY AUTOBIOGRAPHY

With Jacob Steinberg

HarperCollins*Publishers*

HarperCollins*Publishers*
1 London Bridge Street
London SE1 9GF

www.harpercollins.co.uk

HarperCollins*Publishers*
Macken House, 39/40 Mayor Street Upper
Dublin 1, D01 C9W8, Ireland

First published by HarperCollins 2022
This edition published 2023

1 3 5 7 9 10 8 6 4 2

A catalogue record of this book is
available from the British Library

ISBN 978-0-00-853134-8

Printed and bound in the UK using 100%
renewable electricity at CPI Group (UK) Ltd

Contents

Introduction

Sometimes I wonder if it was written in the stars. For almost two decades I had the privilege of playing for my boyhood club, and I feel nothing but gratitude when I look back on my journey. West Ham mean the world to me and while there have been plenty of bumps along the way – relegation from the Premier League in 2011, agonising defeats in cup competitions, the wrench of leaving Upton Park – even the difficult times will never change how much it meant to me, that little east London lad who walked home after making his debut, to have spent my entire career in claret and blue.

This was my destiny and I would not have had it any other way. If people see me as a dying breed, the last of the one-club men, then that's easy to understand. I have had claret and blue blood running through my veins all my life and it's difficult to imagine playing for anyone other than West Ham. How could it be anyone else? I was born into a family of Hammers and spent my childhood wearing West Ham kits, having West Ham birthdays and dreaming of following in the footsteps of superstars like Joe Cole, Michael Carrick, Rio Ferdinand and Frank Lampard.

It felt like I was coming home when I left Arsenal's academy and got my move to West Ham when I was 11. The bonus was that the club would give their youth players two free tickets to home games. They put us in the West Stand at Upton Park, and enough time has probably passed for me to be able to admit that I would try to sneak a few mates in for free, squeezing them through the turnstiles before the stewards could stop us.

We were always trying our luck. West Ham had no idea that they were responsible for our pocket money. My mate had a girlfriend who worked in one of the kiosks at Upton Park and we knew that she would look after us. The deal was incredible: we gave her £5 for a burger and a Coke, and she gave us £20 back in change, which might explain why West Ham never seemed to have enough money to buy new players.

They were great times. I loved going to Upton Park and hearing 'I'm Forever Blowing Bubbles' strike up when the teams walked out before kick-off. It was a special place, although it did have an edge. The atmosphere was intimidating when certain teams came to town, and being in the academy did not stop me from occasionally getting a bit carried away. I was a fan when I was with my mates, and although it's not like we were auditioning for parts in *Green Street*, I do look back and laugh at how we behaved as teenagers. Trouble was waiting if you wanted to find it, and our group found that out when I went to Upton Park with a big group of lads for a game against Millwall in 2003, only to end up standing in the doorway of a shop and wondering if I'd made the biggest mistake of my life.

What was I thinking? I certainly wasn't feeling particularly brave as a group of Millwall fans marched down the street and I saw this big West Ham fan turn round and shout, 'No one go anywhere, no one walk away, stand firm!' It was a big reality check. You think you're a hard man at that age, you think you can take on the world, but to be honest I just felt like a little boy as I looked at my mate and thought, 'Oh my God, we're going to get killed here.'

Luckily I lived to tell the tale and the club never found out about my days as a wannabe hooligan. It was pretty stupid behaviour. I didn't need to get involved with that stuff. Going to the football should have been enough of a thrill for me. I loved watching our cheeky midfielder John Moncur, who would entertain the crowd by pulling down the linesman's shorts when he was warming up as a substitute, and I idolised Paolo Di Canio. He was brilliantly skilful, and one of my best memories was having an inadvertent training session with him when I was only 13.

It came about because me and my mate Nicky, who was also in the academy, used to get the 173 bus down to the training ground at Chadwell Heath for a kickabout if we didn't have to train on a Saturday. We thought that we could do what we wanted, and our presence didn't seem to bother anybody. We could even count on the kit-man to make sure we were wearing proper training gear, and our impromptu sessions paid off when, much to our astonishment, Di Canio spotted us while he was getting treatment from his physio and came over to play with us.

We couldn't believe it, and thankfully we managed to hold our own. Hearing Di Canio say he couldn't believe our technique for young kids was one of the best moments of my life. It was all we could talk about on the coach home. Imagine what it was like for a couple of kids to get that kind of praise from Di Canio. 'I want to be a footballer so bad,' I thought. 'So bad.'

It had given me a taste, but the standards at West Ham were so high. I looked up to Joe Cole, who was a few years above me in the academy. I was a ball boy when West Ham thrashed Coventry City in the FA Youth Cup final in 1999, with Joe stealing the show, and I remember sitting near him during a game against Middlesbrough earlier in the tournament. Joe wasn't playing and he caught me off guard when he heard me praising Middlesbrough's No10.

'He wouldn't get near me if I was on the pitch,' Joe said.

I just exchanged awestruck looks with my dad, taking it all in, and realised how much I still had to learn. 'That's the sort of confidence I've got to have to make it,' I thought. 'That's the sort of self-belief I've got to have.'

Yet I had a different character to Joe. I was a shy kid and I never really had his self-confidence. One of my biggest strengths was my drive. I was ready to give everything I had to play for West Ham. They were my second family. It was about soul and belonging. I was a local boy, a West Ham fanatic, and I didn't want anything to stop my dream from becoming a reality. It mattered too much to me. After all I only lived round the corner.

1

Claret and Blue Blood

Growing up in east London meant that West Ham were in my blood. My life was all about football when I was young. My earliest memory is living on Jenkins Road, opposite the fire station in Plaistow, and having a playing field backing on to our house. My dad Mark cut a small square in the back fence to let us through, then used a spanner to open up the metal barrier blocking access to what would become my first football pitch, and once the path was clear everyone in the area used to go there to play football after school.

They were special times. Robert Hatton, one of my team-mates from those games, is still one of my best friends. He lived near our school in Custom House, Rosetta Primary School, and nobody could separate us. My routine was that I would get up, head to the corner shop to buy a Milky Bar because I was under the impression that white chocolate was healthy, then put my life at risk by running across the A13 and knock on Robert's door so we could have a quick kickabout before school.

I loved it, and it wasn't long before I started to realise that I was good at football. I could feel it when I got the ball in the playground, dribbled past all my opponents and scored. It was obvious that I had something extra, and my first taste of proper football came when my mate Bradley's dad saw me playing on the field one day. 'Mark's pretty good,' he said to my old man. 'Do you want to bring him down to training for Barking Colts?'

I didn't need a second invitation. I was only eight – Bradley was a couple of years older than me – but I wanted to test myself. I went along for training and didn't look back. The only problem was that the guy in charge said he didn't have space for any more players. Bradley's dad had to convince the coach to make room for me and I made sure his generosity did not go to waste, playing well enough to convince Barking to sign me up.

Little did I know that my career was now under way. I was, however, obsessed with improving my game. I just loved playing football and was focused on succeeding at Barking. I enjoyed going to training and I was buzzing when they asked me to play in my first five-a-side tournament. I was so excited, although my emotions must have been all over the place, given that the first thing I did when the game kicked off was take the ball and start taking players on, only to realise that I was running in the wrong direction and was heading towards my own goal.

I have no idea what I was doing. Dad was baffled on the sidelines but nobody gave me a hard time about it. Playing for Barking was great, even though we weren't particularly good, because I had all my mates there. It was different when I started to play for a team called Lakeview. I didn't know anyone and, although I was the best player, I felt like none of my team-mates wanted to pass me the ball.

Did they not like me? It feels stupid now, but I was quite insecure about how people perceived me when I was younger. I was nervous about meeting new people and I needed some convincing when I had an opportunity to leave Lakeview for Heath Park & Redbridge. I sat on the edge of Mum and Dad's bed, worrying about what would happen if the other boys didn't take to me, and it was a while before I saw sense and agreed to go.

It was the right decision. We had some really good players and won loads of trophies. I was moving in the right direction and it was beginning to dawn on the people around me that I was more talented than the other boys. Dad said he could see that I had a real chance of making it when I was 14. He was always watching over me and I knew that he understood the game. He was a decent player in his day, although I didn't realise how good he was until I saw him play in a dads' game once. He made it look effortless as he repeatedly flicked the ball over the other players. I was blown away by his skill and it made me respect him even more.

Yet Dad wasn't as dedicated as me when he was growing up. His mates say that he was brilliant, but he says he was more interested in going out drinking and trying to impress girls. Eventually he met Mum, and there were bigger things to think about after they had me and my two little sisters, Francesca and Jessica.

Still, there was no attempt from Dad to live his dream through me. He was supportive without being overbearing. He never put any pressure on me to play football, not that I needed much encouragement, and he was never one of those parents who shouted at his kids from the sidelines. That wasn't his style. He stood in the corner on his own, quietly observing the game, and I try to follow his example when I watch my son Lenny play football now.

Dad was always there for me, always ready with a quiet word of advice, and I wanted to be there for him when my parents got divorced. I was 17 and, having just signed my first professional contract at West Ham, I had bought my own flat in Gidea Park. The family dynamic had shifted. My sisters stayed with Mum, while Dad came to live with me for two years because he had nowhere else to go and the divorce settlement meant that he was short of money. It wasn't a burden. Family matters.

*   *   *

My roots mean a lot to me. I was brought up in a tight-knit family and was really close with all of my grandparents, spending a lot of time at their houses. Admittedly I had an ulterior motive. We didn't have a landline at home, so I'd go over to my nan's in the evening and use her phone for free to call my future wife Carly, who I'd started going out with when I was 14.

Everything felt familiar. Aunt Kim and Uncle Tony and their kids, little Toni and James, were close and they went on holiday with us all the time. It feels like everyone has stuck together down the years. It's unbelievable how many links there are between my family and friends. For instance, my sister Frank has had two kids with one of my best mates. My mate Danny had two kids with Carly's best friend Lauren. Carly's sister, Jade, is with someone who was with me in the academy at West Ham.

These ties give me a sense of belonging, a connection with my upbringing. I look back at those times and remember my mum, a big character who knew absolutely everyone in the area, picking us up from school and flying around with seven or eight of us crammed into her old Ford Fiesta. Above all I remember feeling that me and my sisters were in a loving environment, even though we never had much money. I knew that I could count on support from people around me.

Nothing was too much for my parents when it came to my football career. They trekked up and down the country for my games, dragging my poor sisters along with them, and even drove to France when I was selected to play for England in a youth tournament. It wasn't exactly luxury travel. The journey took 12 hours in Dad's work van, a little Citroën Berlingo, and his way of making sure that there was enough room for Mum, my sisters and Carly was to squash a two-seater sofa in the back.

It was absolutely ridiculous, and I knew I was under pressure to make sure their sacrifice didn't count for nothing. Unfortunately there are no guarantees about anything in football – I doubt my family were particularly happy with me when I got myself sent off for a bad tackle after two minutes. It happens. I didn't do it on purpose and nobody needed to tell me I had made a mistake.

Football is such a demanding industry and as I've always been so obsessed with providing for my family I haven't been able to spend enough time with my mum and my sisters. I love them to bits and they mean the world to me, so I'm looking forward to being in their lives more. Frank has two beautiful kids, little Trace and Deana, and I can't wait to spend more time with them.

There was no doubt about my dedication. Football was my life. I wasn't bad academically but my education wasn't my main priority. I was out on the streets as soon as the school day was over, kicking balls against fences and taking my mates on in the park, and I wouldn't go home until it was time for bed. I rarely had dinner at home. A takeaway was fine by me. My diet was absolutely horrendous but I didn't have any worries. I didn't even mind going to bed with muddy knees! It's different for my kids, who have computers to keep them entertained. All we had for company in those days was a football. The streets were where you learnt about life in those days and I think it's why so many footballers come from council estates.

Football was your way of moving up in the world. I was so hungry to experience the adulation of playing for West Ham and the chance to make money also motivated me. I don't think there's a single young player who becomes a professional for the love of football alone. If you have nothing when you're growing up you want more. You want to have nicer things and provide for your family.

But it takes immense dedication to reach that level. I didn't let my talent go to my head and I didn't have outside distractions. It helps that Carly has always been by my side. Our mums went to school together and our families were close. Carly was always around and, thinking that I was a bit of a gentleman, I eventually plucked up the courage to ask her out.

There was only problem. We went for a Chinese meal on Barking Road and everything was going well until I realised that I had no money on me, which probably wasn't the best first impression. But Carly didn't mind paying. She was already working for her uncle, who had shoe shops up and down the country. I rarely saw her at school. She didn't like it and was happier working, so she always had money.

Carly was so generous. She bought me trainers for school and got me a nice watch. She even bought my first ever suit. I knew she had my back and I didn't like being away from her. I even had mixed feelings when I got called up by England's Under-16s for the first time. The tournament was in Ballymena, Northern Ireland, and I didn't want to leave Carly behind. We'd only been going out for a month but it was a strange feeling. It didn't feel right without Carly, and my mood didn't improve when I broke my foot during the tournament. It was an early reminder that football is a demanding job. You have to be ready to make sacrifices.

*   *   *

Some kids can't cope with the pressure of being in an academy. There are so many skilful youngsters but you need to have the right mentality. I played with a lot of talented footballers at Sunday League level and the percentage who make it is so small. You have to stay level-headed, so I'm fortunate that I've always had a placid personality.

Give me a ball and somewhere to play: that's all I wanted. I even ended up making up the numbers by playing as a ringer for the opposition when I went to watch my mate Shorty play one Sunday afternoon. There was no holding back. I scored six goals in a 7-1 win and during the game I could hear parents from the losing team complaining about me. They didn't know who I was and I felt pretty bad given that Shorty's parents, Tina and Gary, were like a second mum and dad to me. I wasn't trying to humiliate anyone. I grew up with Shorty and spent so many summers in Cyprus with his family. Once the ball was at my feet, though, I couldn't help myself. I even kept playing for my school team when I was at West Ham. The club weren't happy about it but Dad backed me up. 'Look,' he said. 'Unless he plays for his school, he ain't playing for you.'

West Ham weren't in the mood for an argument, though it's unlikely that I actually would have left had it come to it.

I was ecstatic when I joined West Ham as an 11-year-old, with Arsenal fighting a losing battle to convince me to stay with them. I had no ill feeling towards them, as they'd signed me when I was nine. They made their move after scouting me at Barking Colts and everything happened very quickly. They treated me brilliantly and I had a great education under the former Arsenal midfielder Liam Brady. He was a brilliant youth coach and I had no complaints about the set-up there. I met stars like Paul Merson and Dennis Bergkamp, while the academy was full of good players. We had Bradley Johnson, who went on to play for Norwich in the Premier League, and Colin Kazim-Richards, who played for Turkey at Euro 2008. I already knew Bradley and Colin after playing against them at Sunday League level, so settling in at Arsenal wasn't a problem. The issue was the journey from east to north London. Dad drove me after work and I was always late because of traffic – so this made it even easier to join West Ham when my contract with Arsenal was up.

It was the right call. West Ham were known as the Academy of Football because of the players who had come off their production line, and the coaches were fantastic. We were given a solid grounding. People like Tony Carr, Paul Heffer and Peter Brabrook were strong but fair, and made sure we kept our feet on the ground by giving us plenty of menial jobs to do.

It was tough love. Coaches could be harder with kids in those days, but there was still plenty of support. I hit it off with Paul Heffer and Kevin Keen, kept moving through the ranks and knew that Tony Carr, who had a huge reputation after leading the development of Joe Cole, Michael Carrick, Jermain Defoe, Frank Lampard and Rio Ferdinand, had my back. Tony always pushed me to play above my age group, and I realised that things were getting serious when I was 14 and Dad called my school to deliver an urgent message from West Ham.

It was an incredible moment. I was close with my PE teacher Mr Foster, who loved Southampton, and always went to his office when I got into trouble. We'd sit there chatting away about football and I loved playing for him. We won loads of trophies at school – we even played tournaments at Stamford Bridge and Wembley – and it had to be Mr Foster who came into my classroom to tell me that West Ham had called Dad to say that they needed me to play a reserve game against Leicester City at Dagenham & Redbridge's ground that night.

I couldn't believe it. This was a different level to academy football: reserve matches featured first-team players who were out in the cold or recovering from injury. I played alongside Don Hutchison, an experienced pro who was making his way back from a torn cruciate, and felt so nervous sitting in the dressing room before the game. 'What am I doing here?' I thought. 'I don't belong here.'

The game went by in a blur. I wish I'd made more of the experience, especially as I was the youngest player to play a reserve match for West Ham until Jayden Fevrier broke my record in 2018. All the same I knew I was moving in the right direction. Our youth team was strong, aggressive and technically gifted. We won the Nike Cup two years in a row, and went to tournaments in Berlin and Lisbon.

My game was progressing. I was a skilful, energetic, box-to-box midfielder who liked to get on the ball and pick a pass. I was suited to playing for West Ham and the coaches rated me. Opportunities continued to come my way. Another arrived when the late Glenn Roeder, who was manager of the first team at the time, rang my home to ask me to train with the first team while school was on half-term.

I had to pinch myself and didn't say much before training began. I was only 15 and was training in the indoor gym at Chadwell Heath with John Moncur, Paolo Di Canio, Trevor Sinclair and Joe Cole. I was lost for words when Dad picked me up at the end of the day. I was a tiny little thing but I hadn't disgraced myself in front of my idols. I had clipped a ball over the top for Trevor to score a nice goal and I could tell the players were impressed.

The nerves disappeared once I was on the pitch. I held my own in the keep-ball sessions and there was plenty of encouragement. None of the players knew my name but football's a common language and it doesn't take long to work out if someone is good enough.

'Well done, little man.'

'Good pass.'

I felt they accepted me and I was desperate to experience more. Soon, though, the stars were on their way out.

It was horrible when West Ham were relegated from the Premier League in May 2003. The club was in financial trouble and supporters were devastated when Joe, Paolo, Trevor, Freddie Kanouté, Defoe and Glen Johnson left. We had to rebuild in the Championship, though dropping into the second tier probably had a good impact on my career. It meant there were more opportunities to be around the first team during the 2003–04 season, and I was asked to travel to a few away games with the squad after Alan Pardew replaced Glenn Roeder as manager. Of course, you don't say anything at that age. You just want approval from the adults. We'd be on the coach for hours and I spent a lot of those journeys making cups of tea for David James, who was England's No1.

It wasn't about football; it was about showing respect. The first team was full of experienced players and I was nowhere near proving that I belonged. Being part of the travelling party is one thing, but it was a long way from playing for the first team, so I was incredibly envious when Pards handed my mate Chris Cohen his senior debut in

December 2003. 'I want that so bad,' I thought. 'I need to play in the first team.'

I played with Chris in the academy and was happy to see him make the next step. He had bigger legs than me and was further along in his development. He was a cracking player and went on to have a very good career for Nottingham Forest. There were no hard feelings when I saw him playing for the first team; I was close with Chris and thought that West Ham made a big error when they sold him to Yeovil Town in 2005.

Nonetheless I didn't like the feeling of being left behind. Chris was getting chances to play with Michael Carrick, whereas I was still making tea on the team coach. It made me even hungrier. I had to convince Pardew to give me a chance. I was desperate for a taste of the real thing.

Patience was key. It was clear that the first-team coaches rated me, given that I travelled with the first team when they went to Cardiff to play Crystal Palace in the play-off final in 2004. I was in the thick of it, although I still had to prove myself to the lads. What's more, Chris and I were terrified when we were told we had to do initiation songs on the eve of the final. We hid away in our room for a while, and even considered creeping out of the hotel and catching a train back to London. 'I just don't want to sing,' I thought, but I eventually realised there was no way out. In the end Chris picked an Oasis song and, not knowing much about music, I chose the song closest to my heart. 'I'll just sing "Bubbles",' I thought, praying that the players would sing along to West Ham's anthem. Fat chance, though. They absolutely hammered me and I wanted the ground to swallow me whole.

The next day wasn't much better. I was gutted when I watched us miss out on an instant return to the Premier League after losing 1–0 to Palace at the Millennium Stadium. The mood around the club was low and the fans were worried about the future. Were we ever going to make it back?

Not that I was overly concerned. Young players are care-free and I didn't feel any pressure because of the club's situation. It's not your fault if the team's struggling. The fans don't blame you for bad results, and my main thought during pre-season was whether I could make my break-through and help West Ham win promotion. 'They're the best times,' I tell kids now. 'You've got no pressure, so go out and play. You're lucky to get this opportunity, so just grab it with both hands.' That's what I had to do. I just needed a chance to come my way.

* * *

I didn't realise that the stars had all aligned when we lost to Palace. We'd have been a Premier League team if we'd won and Pardew would have had money to spend on new players during the summer. He wouldn't have had to think about using kids like me, so my pathway would have been blocked. I'd have carried on playing for the youth team or been sent out on loan to gain experience. But sometimes it's a case of right time, right place in football.

The club's disappointment about missing out on promotion worked in my favour. It's why I think I was destined to play for West Ham. I wanted the best for them but I saw their lowest moment as an opportunity. So what if money was tight? I was too young to worry about the balance sheet, and if the manager didn't have funds to build a complete squad then that would only increase my chances of breaking into the first team.

That had to be my aim at the start of the 2004–05 season, even if West Ham were expected to push for promotion again. 'Please call me over,' I thought when I saw Chris Cohen with the senior players. 'Please let me train with the first team.'

Soon my prayers were answered. Pards brought me into the fold before the start of the campaign and I quickly settled in. We had signed Teddy Sheringham on a free transfer from Portsmouth and he saw something in me straight away. 'Wee man, I'm really liking your touch,' he said after one session, which was music to my ears. I was straight on the phone to Dad to tell him about the nice things Teddy was saying about me. It meant so much. Teddy was coming towards the end of his career but he commanded so much respect. He was a top striker, had helped Manchester United win the Champions League and held sway with Pards. 'You've got to play him,' Teddy said to the manager about me. 'The way he's training, you've got to put him in.'

Luckily Pards valued Teddy's input. He took the advice on board and my dream was closer to becoming a reality when Jimmy Hampson, Head of Academy Recruitment, came over to talk to me and Dad. 'I've just had a message from the first team,' Jimmy said. 'Mark's in the squad for the Crewe game.'

It was a huge moment. We'd made a slow start to the season, picking up four points from our first three games, and a few players were out. The fans were grumbling and we needed a result when we travelled north to play Crewe, though my main focus was making sure not to step on anyone's toes. I was still only 17 and you don't want to say anything to anyone at that stage. I just sat on the bench at Gresty Road, taking it all in as two goals from Teddy and one from Rufus Brevett saw us go 3–0 up inside the first 30 minutes.

Unfortunately Crewe hit back with two goals and we were hanging on for the win at the end. It wasn't the right time for Pards to throw me in. I had to be patient. Another opportunity was waiting round the corner. I was on the bench again when we hosted Southend United in the first round of the League Cup three days later and this time I was confident that Pards would put me on. He wanted to see what our young players were made of and started three of my academy mates: Trent McClenahan, Chris Cohen and Elliot Ward. It wasn't as big as a league game and Southend were two divisions below us.

I was ready. The only disappointment was that Mum and Dad had booked a holiday to Cyprus with my sisters and couldn't be at Upton Park. It was gutting for them but at least Carly was with me. It was thanks to her that I looked the part. We had to wear a suit to the game and I was in a Hugo Boss one she bought for me before an England youth game. It was off the rack and it wasn't made to fit, but I wasn't complaining. I just wanted to get on the pitch.

It didn't feel real. Six months earlier I'd been waiting outside the ground, asking players for autographs after games. I still lived at home and all my mates were Hammers. Now I was about to live out their dream.

I had so many people at the game, even though Mum, Dad and my sisters weren't there. The club gave us free tickets in the West Stand and I gave them to Carly, my mate and Dad's friends. It was a proud moment for our community and my heart was racing when Pards turned round midway through the second half and told me to get ready.

'I'm coming on,' I thought as I removed my tracksuit top. 'I can't believe it.' I could barely concentrate. I could see the faces in the crowd but it passed by in a blur. 'This is what I want in life,' I thought. 'These are the moments I want.'

I didn't care about the result. We were 1–0 up when I came on for Luke Chadwick but I just wanted to savour the moment. I'd played at Upton Park in the FA Youth Cup but this was a different level. There were only 17,000 fans there – it was a midweek game against a lower-league side in August – but it felt like 170,000 to me. The adrenaline was pumping and it felt even more surreal when Pards brought Teddy on for Sergei Rebrov with 14 minutes to go. 'Bloody hell,' I thought. 'I'm on the same pitch as Teddy Sheringham.'

It was beautiful. The game finished 2–0 to us and I was buzzing when we walked off the pitch. I had so many messages, and I managed to call Mum and Dad to tell them I'd made my debut. My brain was swimming, and it hadn't occurred to me that I didn't have a way of getting home. I didn't have a driving licence and Dad wasn't there to give me a lift. 'F**k it,' I said to Carly. 'Let's just walk home.'

I'd done that walk back to Beckton so many times: straight down through East Ham, past Brampton School, down the A13, over the Blue Bridge and through my front door. It took 25 minutes at most and I didn't think twice about doing it after making my debut. It felt natural.

I didn't realise that people would look at me differently now. I was wearing my Hugo Boss suit and I wasn't prepared for two middle-aged men to spot me in the street. 'Well done, Marky boy,' one shouted. 'Oh my God, Mark,' Carly said as we walked on. 'He knew who you were.'

My life had changed, although I was yet to realise it. We had a Chinese takeaway when we got home and I just wanted to go out on the street to play another game. Loads of my mates were out and I spent the night standing outside my house, chatting to them about becoming a West Ham footballer.

It was incredible and I was still on top of the world when I went to training the next day. There was no jealousy from the other academy boys. Darren Blewitt, who supported West Ham, was delighted for me. I could feel that everyone was proud of me. They knew how much it meant.

Deep down, though, I still wasn't satisfied. Those 20 minutes against Southend weren't enough. I wanted the good press and the adulation. I wanted to be rich and successful. I had a taste but I was still hungry. I had to have another bite.

2

Growing Pains

I was never going to stop after making my debut. Once the euphoria passed I told myself not to let anything get in my way. I was going to dedicate my life to football. There was no other option. I didn't want any distractions. I wasn't lured in by the bright lights of London and I didn't care if I upset anyone.

Fortunately the people around me understood who I was. I would do anything for my family and friends, but they'd have to accept that I'm a nightmare when things go badly on the pitch. I hate losing and I go into my shell after defeats. West Ham have always surrounded me. Sometimes it means too much and the older I got, the more the pressure to perform grew.

As a 17-year-old kid, though, my only concern was myself. I moved into that flat on my own in Gidea Park and could have gone partying with my mates, but they never tried to lead me astray. They knew they'd have been wasting their time. I wasn't interested in nights out. They'd get ready to go out on a Friday and I'd be tucked up in bed, making sure I was rested for Saturday afternoon.

Carly was supportive. She wasn't particularly interested in football but knew what it meant to me. She didn't worry about our social life. She was already so responsible and didn't mind if we stayed in. She was working so hard at her uncle's shop and I was adamant that my gifts weren't going to go to waste.

I knew there was still much to prove after the Southend game. It was a brief cameo and there were plenty of experienced midfielders in front of me. Pards had Nigel Reo-Coker, Hayden Mullins, Carl Fletcher and Steve Lomas. I was at the back of the queue and I wasn't even on the bench for our next game, a 1–0 home win over Burnley in the league. It was frustrating. I was left out again when we beat Notts County in the third round of the League Cup in September. Self-doubt took hold. I was doing well in the academy but a place in the first-team squad remained elusive.

'I'm never going to be a pro,' I thought in one of my gloomier teenage moments. I wasn't optimistic about my chances of featuring in our next League Cup game. It was away to Chelsea, who had just appointed José Mourinho, and I didn't expect to be involved.

Yet I was being too hard on myself. Despite my disappointment at not playing more, the reality was that Pards was making me feel wanted. I was still training with the first team regularly and I could sense that he liked my game. He'd shown he wasn't scared to play kids and I had a feeling he would give me another chance sooner rather than later.

I just didn't think it would come at Stamford Bridge. I was on the bench again and was blown away by the strength of the Chelsea team. There was no mercy from Mourinho, who started Ricardo Carvalho, Joe Cole and Arjen Robben. We were massive underdogs, and I was desperate to get on the pitch and test myself against Chelsea's stars.

It felt like a distant dream until Pards caught me off guard just before half-time.

'Mark, you're going to come on in the second half. Warm up.'

'What?'

'You're going to come on. Make sure you're warm.'

It was brave management from Pards. We had Don Hutchison on the bench and Pards could have gone for his experience. He didn't have to put me on, especially as Chelsea battered us in the first half. Only brilliant goalkeeping from Jimmy Walker kept us in the game and it wasn't a surprise when Chelsea eventually went ahead early in the second half.

But Pards was true to his word. He believed in me and gave me a push. Chelsea made their first substitution in the 64th minute, replacing Joe Cole with Damien Duff, and we responded a minute later. 'You're coming on,' Pards said. 'This is f**king surreal,' I thought as I replaced Adam Nowland. 'Chelsea away. It's a bit different to Southend.'

It was a fantastic game. Chelsea struggled to kill us off after going 1–0 up. We kept battling, almost snatching a last-minute equaliser when Anton Ferdinand hit the bar, and I got on the ball loads. Southend had gone by in a flash but this felt natural. I made my passes, and I wasn't intimidated when I looked over to the touchline and saw Mourinho bringing on Frank Lampard and Eiður Guðjohnsen. 'Unreal subs,' I thought, but I was determined to play my game and prove that Pards was right to put me on.

Of course, it was harder with Frank on. He was desperate to impress against his old side and looked certain to score when Robben won a penalty late in the second half, only for Jimmy Walker to save Frank's spot-kick with his knees.

The fans loved that one. Dad was at the game and I've got a photo of four of my mates celebrating behind the goal when Frank missed. From my perspective, though, it was simply an honour to play against such a great midfielder. There's a photo of us exchanging shirts after the game and I look like a baby next to him.

My main memory of playing against him was that he always got in the box when Chelsea were on the attack. You'd think you had him, you'd look at the ball for two seconds and by the time you looked back he was already five yards away.

It was such an education. I realised it wasn't a coincidence Frank scored 20 goals a season. I used to think he was lucky when I saw his goals on *Match of the Day*. 'I'm playing in the youth team and I don't even score every week,' I thought, but seeing Frank up close changed my opinion of him. His record wasn't a fluke. It was down to hard work, timing and natural finishing ability. I was a different type of player, a midfielder who wanted to get on the ball and dictate the game, but I had learnt a valuable lesson. You can't switch off.

* * *

It was back to the grind of fighting for promotion after our gutsy defeat at Chelsea. Teams raised their level when they played us, and we struggled to cope. Our form was inconsistent, and instead of challenging for automatic promotion we found ourselves in a battle to make the play-offs.

Yet I wasn't aware if Pards was under pressure from the board. I was young and oblivious. I wasn't worried about the club's dire financial position. I saw an opportunity to get us back where we belonged and I continued to focus on training well. I wasn't arrogant but I was a chirpy character and the other players warmed to me. 'When you train in the first team you have to earn their respect,' I say to the young boys now. 'You can't do anything without it.'

I was showing the right attitude. I made the bench for a couple of league games and was thrown in from the start when we drew Norwich City in the third round of the FA Cup. We were the underdogs once again. They were in the Premier League and had Darren Huckerby and David Bentley, who was on loan from Arsenal. I had reached another milestone. Starting is nothing like coming off the bench, and I was determined not to let Pards down. I played my part and we earned a deserved win when Luke Chadwick set up Marlon Harewood for the only goal.

It was a good cross from Luke, although I was gutted he hadn't picked me out for an easy finish at 0–0. I stayed up all night replaying the chance in my head. 'Why didn't he just play it to my feet?' I thought. 'I'd have had a tap-in.'

But it didn't matter. We were through to the next round and I had played the whole game. Later that evening I was in my parents' room and had a conversation that changed my way of thinking.

'Listen, you're a West Ham player now,' Dad said.

'What do you mean?' I replied. 'That wasn't my first game.'

'No,' Dad said. 'You started today. You're a West Ham player now.'

Those words stayed with me. I was beginning to make my presence felt. The fans wanted me in the team and I started again when we travelled to Wolves in the league a week later. It was another opportunity to learn, with Paul Ince in midfield for them, but a 4–2 defeat left another dent in our promotion challenge and I was taken off near the end.

Pards wasn't sure if he could rely on me yet. I was gutted to be back on the bench when we hosted Derby a week later. The game was live on Sky Sports and my disappointment did not go unnoticed in the dressing room. Our experienced left-back Chris Powell could tell I was upset and he got my head back in the game by leaving a Post-it note on my locker with a simple but incisive message: 'Always be ready.'

It was sound advice from Chris and I kept that Post-it note in my wash bag for years. Young players cannot afford to sulk if a manager leaves them out, and I made sure I was in the right frame of mind before the Derby game. 'Just be ready,' I thought. 'Just in case something happens.'

Sure enough, I was on when Gavin Williams went off injured after seven minutes. I was raring to go thanks to

Chris. I had a really good game and should have had an assist when I sent Marlon through with a great pass, only for Derby's goalkeeper Lee Camp to escape a red card for a last-ditch foul.

Derby were lucky to win 2–1. The ball wouldn't fall for our forwards and we were in danger of slipping out of the play-off picture. We were struggling to put a run together and the mood worsened when we lost 3–1 on penalties away to Sheffield United in the fourth round of the FA Cup.

At least I could hold my head up high. I was also the only player who scored during the shootout and it meant a lot when I got a nod of approval from Steve Lomas on the journey back to London. Steve had captained West Ham and was a top professional. His opinion mattered and it was like he was saying, 'You're all right – I accept you.' He could see I wasn't going to wilt, and although we had lost, I felt unbelievable. 'Do you know what?' I thought. 'I belong here now. And I want to stay here.'

* * *

It was time to fight. We needed to display character during the run-in. Our hopes of making the play-offs were in the balance and I had a setback when I picked up a little injury during a 5–0 win over Plymouth in February. It kept me out for a few games, and although I returned for the trip to Reading in the middle of March, a horrible 3–1 defeat meant our season was threatening to spiral out of control.

A lot of fans wanted Pards out at that stage. We limped on, conceding a last-minute equaliser at home to Crewe, but I was feeling good. I had a great game when we hosted Leicester three days later. It helped that I was developing a good understanding with Teddy, who scored twice in a 2–2 draw. His touch was immaculate and his passes always hit the target. Your level rises when you play with the best and my only disappointment was failing to get on the scoresheet. I went close with a curling shot after a clever lay-off from Teddy and I was unlucky not to score my first goal for the club when I saw a goalbound volley handled on the line by Nikos Dabizas during the dying stages.

I was dying to take the penalty and put us 3–2 up after the referee sent Dabizas off. It would have been mine later down the line. But I was too young to pull rank and I had to stand aside when Marlon stepped up. He had a good record and it was a surprise when he hit a tame effort straight at Ian Walker, whose save left us in increasing danger of failing to finish in the top six.

The margin for error had become virtually non-existent. We were battling with Reading for the final play-off spot and couldn't afford to drop many more points if we were going to finish sixth. The games were running out and the rumours about Pards being sacked were getting louder.

But the board decided to hold off firing him. They chose not to panic and gave him time to come up with a new approach. What we needed was a settled team. Pards knew he had to stop chopping and changing. We needed clarity, and a few simple tweaks helped us settle down. We were more secure once Hayden Mullins wasn't being asked to fill in at right-back. Hayden didn't deserve to be playing out of position and was excellent after moving alongside Nigel Reo-Coker in central midfield. Tomáš Řepka was an obvious alternative on the right, and his tenacity was invaluable as Pards had decided to go for broke by playing a youthful centre-back pairing of Anton Ferdinand and Elliot Ward.

Anton and Elliot were great together. They protected Jimmy Walker, who made a huge impact after replacing Stephen Bywater as our No1 goalkeeper after the Leicester game. I loved Jimmy. He wasn't the tallest but he was a superb shot-stopper and a big character. He used to call me 'King Nobes'. 'You give me a lift when I'm in goal,' Jimmy said. 'Seeing you out there gives me inspiration.'

Something had clicked. Our belief was growing. Shaun Newton was a good signing on a free transfer and gave us balance on the right wing. Teddy, Marlon and Bobby Zamora were top options in attack. We had goals in us and we earned a vital win when we visited Wigan at the start of

April. They were going for automatic promotion but we matched them. Going 1–0 down didn't faze us. Teddy equalised and I set up the winner for Marlon.

It was a turning point. I was playing on the left wing because Matty Etherington was in and out with injuries, and I was in my element when we played Coventry at home. 'Just get the ball to Nobes,' Pards said. 'Let him do the rest.' It was a massive vote of confidence from the manager. He said bringing me into the squad had given everyone a buzz. My enthusiasm was infectious and my love of West Ham lifted the mood.

I was making us tick, although we had to be patient against Coventry. I missed a good chance to put us ahead before the interval and we were relieved when Matty came on during half-time. I moved into central midfield in the second half and Matty, who was a natural left winger, eventually created the winner.

Suddenly promotion felt like a possibility. I was playing for the love of West Ham – my wages weren't big and I wasn't on any promotion bonuses. The tension was high but I relished it. We were building momentum at last and I wanted to savour every moment. I even dreamt about winning promotion. The older lads would never have allowed themselves to be that naive.

The league was tough and uncompromising. Our next game saw us host Millwall at Upton Park and I finished it with a chipped tooth after Kevin Muscat elbowed me at a throw-in. It summed up the game. Millwall fought hard, took the lead and held on for a draw after Marlon equalised.

We had to be more clinical, and my frustration grew when I picked up a minor injury, ruling me out for much of the run-in. Pards had to tweak his approach while I was out and he settled on a new midfield four, with Matty on the left, Nigel and Hayden in the middle, and Shaun on the right. That's football. I got injured at the wrong time and had to watch as others took their chance. Matty was playing really well after shaking off his fitness problems and we snuck into the play-offs on the final day, pipping Reading to sixth place thanks to a 2–1 win away to Watford.

The relief was immense. We had a two-legged semi-final against Ipswich, who had lost out to Sunderland and Wigan in the battle for automatic promotion, and we were determined not to blow it this time.

*   *   *

We knew we were good enough to go up. Ipswich were favourites to reach the final but we raised our level against the big sides. Our problem wasn't a lack of talent, it was our inconsistency. We had blown too many seemingly straightforward games, but the play-offs suited us. We had the firepower to beat anyone. The challenge was making sure we didn't choke under pressure.

It wasn't going to be easy. Ipswich were a strong side and Joe Royle a good manager. They had Jim Magilton pulling the strings in midfield and Darren Bent, a future England forward, was in great goal-scoring form. Shefki Kuqi was another threat up front. Anton and Elliot were going to have their hands full with him.

But we had a good record against Ipswich. We'd taken four points off them during the league campaign and won our semi-final against them a year earlier. They had weaknesses. 'We're going to win these play-offs,' I thought. The excitement was taking over. I was fit again and dared to speculate whether Pards was going to turn to me again. 'I wonder if you'll play me,' I thought before the first leg. 'I wonder if you'll put me back in the team.'

It was wishful thinking. There was no reason for Pards to tweak a winning formula and we came flying out of the traps when Ipswich turned up at Upton Park. They couldn't cope with Matty's pace on the left, and we appeared to be in complete control after going 2–0 up thanks to goals from Marlon Harewood and Bobby Zamora, only for Ipswich to reply with two scrappy goals. We ran out of steam in the second half and I couldn't affect the game after coming on near the end.

Ipswich were the happier side at full-time. A 2–2 draw seemed to put them in the ascendancy given that the second leg was at their place. People were writing us off. Nobody on the outside thought we were going to get a result at Portman Road.

But Pards had a plan. He surprised Ipswich, outnumbering them in midfield by bringing Carl Fletcher in for Shaun Newton. They didn't know how to respond after we switched from a 4–4–2 system to a 4–5–1. We were totally dominant and deservedly went ahead when Bobby tapped in a cross from Marlon at the start of the second half.

Bobby was on fire. He found it difficult to settle at West Ham after leaving Tottenham in 2003, and the fans were on his back at times. When it got serious, though, you could rely on him. When the crunch time arrived it was like he thought, 'Right, I'm going to turn it on now.' He delivered in big moments throughout his career and he was crucial for us during the play-offs, especially as Teddy missed the semi-final with a little injury. Bobby was on Marlon's wavelength and they clicked beautifully when we doubled our lead over Ipswich. Marlon's cross was brilliant and Bobby's first-time volley was absolutely superb.

It was the best possible example of our individual class. It was why I backed us to go up. The lads improved when the heat was on and Ipswich had no way back after going 4–2 down on aggregate. It was over as a contest and I decided that I had to be a part of it. 'Boss!' I said, turning to Pards on the touchline. 'Please put me on.'

His look said one thing: 'You cheeky bastard.' But I had a way of breaking Pards down. 'Go on then,' he said after a brief pause. 'Get your gear off. But you've got to give me £20 every time you give the ball away!'

It was just a bit of banter from Pards. He loved my fearlessness and knew I wasn't nervous. There was only a minute to go but I just wanted to be on the pitch and celebrate in my kit. I had mates in the away end and I wanted to feel that I'd played my part in us reaching the final.

But we couldn't get ahead of ourselves when we travelled to Cardiff for the final. We'd fallen at the last hurdle 12 months earlier, fluffing our lines against Palace, and we still had to finish the job. There was so much riding on it. The club desperately needed promotion and it was up to us to deliver against Preston, who were a good side. They'd done the double over us in the league and were confident of beating us again.

We had to stay calm. Pards was chilled the night before the game and let the lads have a glass of wine. He could see the camaraderie in the group and wanted us to relax. We could tell that promotion was so important to him. We had a boisterous young team and he could see an opportunity to build something if we went up. Our spirit was strong and we were enjoying the journey. People like Bobby lifted the mood. He was going round with a video camera during the days leading up to the game, filming everyone, and managed to catch me slipping over outside the team hotel.

We all had a good laugh at my expense. Obviously my tumble made it into Bobby's DVD, 'Bobby Zamora's Play-off Diary', but I didn't mind. Watching from the bench at the Millennium Stadium, I had no doubt that we were going to beat Preston. We were better than them and went ahead early in the second half. Matty put in a cross, a Preston defender slipped and Bobby was there to score with a cool finish.

It was pandemonium when the ball crept into the net. I was warming up with Teddy and Carl Fletcher when it happened, and was soon sprinting towards the goal to celebrate with Bobby. There's a great photo of me on his back, a picture of pure ecstasy. We were on our way and, having never played in a stadium that big before, I couldn't believe how loud the roar from the crowd was when we scored.

It meant so much to the fans, who had seen so many great players leave after relegation. It meant so much to me. The thought of going up had consumed me for weeks and I was ready when Pards put me on with eight minutes left. I'll never forget that from him. It was a massive decision to put an 18-year-old novice on at such an important stage. I owe Pards a lot for trusting in me. Not all managers are that brave when it comes to using academy players.

But I had to remember that I wasn't coming on for a party. The game wasn't over yet. Jimmy Walker came off his line to collect a long ball, misjudged his positioning and landed outside his penalty area. For a moment it looked like he was going to be sent off for handball. Even more worryingly, Jimmy had twisted his knee in an attempt to stay inside the box. He was lying on the turf in agony, and although he escaped a red card he had to be replaced by Stephen Bywater.

Thankfully Stephen saved the resulting free-kick. We survived, and the feeling when the final whistle went was unforgettable. I was running round the pitch with my shirt on back to front, a scarf draped round my head and a West Ham flag wrapped around my waist. Up in the stands Jimmy Hampson, Head of Academy Recruitment, was quick to congratulate Dad. 'Your boy's a Premier League player now,' Jimmy said. 'I could feel the tears rolling down my cheeks,' Dad told me. 'It was incredible.'

I was just as emotional. It was such a rapid rise. I had only just left school and now I was going to play in the Premier League. The joy was overwhelming. I laughed, I cried and I drank it all in. I watched the fans celebrating in the stands and I didn't want it to end. I was a West Ham fan, a kid who grew up round the corner, and I couldn't believe I'd played a part in my boyhood club winning promotion.

Going up changes a footballer's life. We were all in line for pay rises, so it wasn't a surprise that the dressing room was bouncing. The beers were out and everyone was singing and dancing, although I hadn't even thought about the money. I was on around £2,500 a week, which was good for an 18-year-old, but my agent was already plotting. 'We're negotiating as a Premier League player now,' he said.

It makes a big difference. At that stage, though, I just wanted to savour the moment. There were celebrations back at the hotel and the club arranged a promotion parade when we returned to London a day later. We took an open-top bus from Barking Road to Upton Park and were amazed by how many fans came out to greet us. The streets were heaving and I felt another stab of pride when I spotted mates from school in the crowd. I couldn't stop smiling. I had the trophy in one hand and a West Ham flag in the other. Life could not have been better.

*   *   *

The mood around the club was brilliant after promotion. We had an energetic young team and we wanted to attack the Premier League. Obviously pundits wrote us off at the start of the season, but we were fearless and fancied our chances of surprising people. If they underestimated us that was their problem. We had more than enough talent to avoid relegation and Pards was proactive during pre-season, improving the squad with a few canny signings. Danny Gabbidon and James Collins were strong buys in central defence, and we were excited about the arrival of Yossi Benayoun, a classy Israeli midfielder with bundles of creativity and an eye for goal.

I loved playing with Yossi. He was a cracking player and a great guy. Pards was raising our level and we were brilliant on the opening day of the season, coming back from a goal down to beat Blackburn 3–1 at home. 'I want this now,' I thought after coming off the bench with six minutes left. 'This is where I've got to play now.'

I assumed I was going to be part of Pards's plans. But I was young. I was still developing and filling out. I was a long way from my physical peak and I was frustrated after picking up a muscle problem, which left me watching from the sidelines as the boys continued to perform well without me.

I had to stay calm. I worked my way back to fitness and focused on training well. There was no point sulking, and an opening emerged when Nigel Reo-Coker picked up an injury at the start of November. 'You're playing this weekend,' Pards said. 'Make sure you're ready.'

'Oh wow,' I thought. 'It's Tottenham away.'

I was straight on the phone to Dad. 'You're not going to believe it,' I said. 'I'm playing this weekend.'

'No way.'

'I'm telling you, Dad. The gaffer told me I'm playing.'

It was the first time in my career I had ever felt proper nerves. I was in the away end at White Hart Lane when we visited Spurs in 2002, celebrating like mad when Ian Pearce equalised with a last-minute volley from 25 yards. Nobody needed to tell me about the rivalry. I was full of adrenaline and couldn't wait to test myself against a really good side.

The odds were against us. Spurs were going for Champions League qualification and had Edgar Davids, Jermaine Jenas and Michael Carrick in midfield. It was a daunting challenge. I trained with Michael when he was at West Ham and was staggered by his quality. It was obvious that he was going to play for a top side. He was like a luxury car: big, tall and strong, and his passing was second to none.

But I wasn't intimidated. I always loved playing against Spurs, even though we took some awful hidings off them at times. I had some great games against them and didn't mind the abuse from their fans. I wasn't bothered about being called a pikey and them telling me to go back to my caravan. I shrugged it off when a burger full of tomato sauce hit me on the back of the neck as I was preparing to take a corner at White Hart Lane on one occasion.

You just had to laugh and give it back when you had the chance. All my mates hated Spurs, but that's football. A few years later I was on holiday in Mauritius and met a guy called Steve Flashman. He was a massive Spurs fan and wouldn't talk to me at first, even though his wife Nancy was good friends with one of Carly's aunts. Steve hated West Ham and wasn't happy because I was starting for England Under-21s instead of Tom Huddlestone, who played for Spurs.

There was no getting through to Steve. He blanked me at breakfast and he only mellowed down after Nancy came over to Carly for a chat. 'I'm really good friends with Nicki,' she said. 'She lives on the same road as me.' Steve had to open up and we're mates now. His WhatsApp photo is a picture of himself lying on a sofa at my house in a Spurs shirt, but I got my own back when we were on holiday in Florida. Steve was livid when he saw that I'd put an Arsenal cap on his little boy's head. He threw the hat in a fountain and didn't talk to me for the rest of the day.

That's football fans for you. I'd have been the same if I hadn't become a professional, and I was dying to do well after Pards threw me in at the deep end against Spurs. 'I

don't want to let anyone down,' I thought. 'Spurs away ...
I've dreamt of this moment.'

It was a big test. It was my first Premier League start and
I was blown away by the pace of the game at first. After
spending the first 10 minutes catching my breath, though,
I began to feel more at ease. I made my presence felt with
a proper tackle on Davids and was unlucky to have a goal
ruled out for offside.

I didn't feel out of place. We held our own after going
1–0 down and the celebrations were manic when Anton
equalised in the last minute. Our fans went crazy and I was
delighted to have helped us earn a point. 'Nobes, you
showed some f**king bollocks today,' Pards said. 'You
struggled in the first 10 minutes, but you grew into the
game and showed some balls. Well done.'

But a reality check was on the way. I learnt a valuable
lesson when I started against Manchester United at Upton
Park a week later. Marlon gave us an early lead but I
couldn't get in the game. I didn't believe I belonged in the
Premier League yet and I definitely wasn't ready to take on
United, who came back to win 2–1.

They were too good for us. Gary Neville came on
midway through the first half and changed the game from
right-back. I hadn't seen anyone do that before and I
couldn't get close to Paul Scholes in midfield. He was one
of my hardest ever opponents. Every time you tried to

press him he'd lay the ball off. Eventually I decided that I was going to stand off but as soon as that happened he started playing 60-yard passes.

There was no way of breaking his control of the game. I didn't play terribly, but I still had a lot to learn. I had gone from playing youth football to taking on United in no time at all and it was inevitable that my inexperience was going to catch up with me. I struggled when we won 2–1 at Birmingham. I wasn't ready. I played again when we visited Blackburn, but it didn't go well. It was a rude awakening. I was a bit full of myself during the warm-up. I looked at Tugay, who had grey hair and a ponytail, and thought I'd outplay him. I assumed that Robbie Savage just went around kicking people.

What was I thinking? Tugay and Savage were experienced Premier League midfielders and they gave me a footballing lesson. I felt like a 12-year-old and Pards took me off after an hour. We lost 3–2 and I couldn't blame Pards for losing faith in me. He gave me a chance and I wasn't able to repay him.

Football is brutal at that level. Pards no longer trusted me and I didn't play again for West Ham that season. I was too innocent and the situation didn't improve when I joined Hull on loan after Christmas. They were in the Championship and I wanted to give it a go but it wasn't a good fit. The atmosphere felt alien and I was too embarrassed to tell anyone when I hurt my back during my first training session.

It was a terrible way to start. Hull's manager Peter Taylor wanted me in his team but I didn't feel like the other players respected me. I sensed they saw me as a flash kid from London and I could tell that one of my fellow midfielders didn't like me. There were times when I'd try to bring the ball down and play, only to hear him screaming at me to get it forward as quickly as possible.

I found it baffling. My way was to get the ball on the floor and pick out a team-mate. It was difficult and I found it difficult to settle. Peter Taylor treated me well and I played a few games, but I didn't enjoy it. I was staying in a hotel and there were times when I wondered if it was worth the hassle. 'If I'm giving up my family life and my mates to come and live up here on my own, this is not what I want,' I thought. 'This is not what I thought being a professional footballer was going to be about.'

It was the worst time of my career. I was an absolute nobody up there and I hated it. It's why I always tried to make loan players feel comfortable at West Ham. I didn't have that, and the biggest positive from my time with Hull was that it made me even more determined to play for West Ham, where I knew I was loved.

I just wanted to come back. I travelled back to London as much as possible to see Carly and eventually decided I had to tell Pards that it wasn't working out. 'My back's killing me,' I said. 'You have to bring me back.'

Pards was sceptical at first. 'You're just saying that because it isn't here,' he replied. 'You've got to get over it. You've got to tough it out.'

But I refused to budge. I forced my way back and breathed a sigh of relief. I was home again, and although I didn't play again all season, I loved watching the boys finish ninth in the Premier League and reach the FA Cup final. I travelled with the squad when we went to Cardiff to face Liverpool in the final and was watching from the stands when Steven Gerrard broke my heart with his stunning last-minute equaliser. It was so sad. We didn't deserve to lose on penalties, but what can you do about a Stevie G masterclass? 'That's the level I've got to get to,' I thought, looking at Liverpool's world-class captain. 'That's the standard.'

3

The Great Escape

I was jealous of the boys during their run to the FA Cup final. I watched from the sidelines, willing them on, kicking every ball, but it hurt not to be involved. It was the first time I'd felt like an outsider at West Ham, and the reality of the situation wasn't lost on me at the start of the 2006–07 season. I clearly wasn't in Alan Pardew's plans and I knew that I couldn't afford to spend the next few months just kicking my heels.

I wasn't prepared to let my career hit a brick wall, although I was careful not to let anything jeopardise my chances of succeeding at West Ham. I was savvy enough to know there was nothing to be gained from rushing into the manager's office to ask for a transfer, which was the last thing on my mind. All I needed was regular first-team football and the only way to get it was by going out on loan again.

I didn't blame Pards. I loved playing for him when I broke into the team and he made me feel like I was walking on water at times. He did so much for my career but he also had to look after his own interests. Football can change in an instant and managers know they can get sacked after one bad run. Their job depends on making the right calls and if Pards didn't feel he could rely on me, then who was I to complain? I was just a kid and I hadn't taken my chance in the Premier League. If Pards had lost faith in me then I had to look at myself in the mirror and work out where I was going wrong.

Players should be more willing to admit when they're playing badly. It's rare for anyone to go into the manager's office, hold their hands up and say they're letting the team down. It usually goes the other way. Players love to make excuses for their poor form. They say the manager's tactics are wrong. They say it's because a team-mate's making them look bad. Or they claim they're not in the team because the coach is singling them out.

But you have to be ready to take responsibility for your own performances. I understood why Pards wasn't picking me and I knew there was no point whinging. It wasn't going to make me a better player. It was up to me to challenge myself and step out of my comfort zone, so I didn't hesitate when Ipswich asked to take me on a three-month loan at the start of the season.

It was a better fit than Hull. Ipswich are a fantastic club and we had a good young team. I had no concerns about settling in this time. I knew Simon Walton from the England youth set-up, Dean Bowditch and Billy Clark were welcoming, and I was pleased to be reunited with Gavin Williams, who had just joined Ipswich from West Ham.

I always had a laugh with Gav. He was a cracking midfielder but he was also a complete lunatic. You never knew what he was going to do next. There was the time we went for a night out in Essex and Gav volunteered to be the designated driver, which suited me perfectly until I woke up while we were driving home during the early hours and realised that a man and a woman wearing backpacks were sitting next to me in the back of the car.

'Gav, what the f**k are you doing?' I said.

'I just thought it would be good banter,' he replied.

What could you say? That was Gav: he saw nothing wrong with picking up a couple of hitchhikers on the A12 in the middle of the night. It was hard to be annoyed with him. He was always making people laugh and I loved spending time with him.

They were great days. I was staying in a house in the centre of town and I quickly hit it off with the other lads.

Ipswich is a small place but we weren't bothered. We were never short of entertainment. You could always find us in the betting shop after training, whiling away the hours in the afternoon by playing on the fruit machine or having a flutter on the horses, and we ate together every night.

The contrast with my time at Hull was enormous. I was happy at Ipswich, I wasn't far from Essex and there were times when I thought about joining them permanently if West Ham didn't want me. I liked my team-mates and the manager, Jim Magilton, was superb with me. Jim, who was in his first management job, taught me a lot. He smoothed out the rough edges to my game and because he had been a technical midfielder before retiring I think he believed in my style of play, which gave me the belief to express myself on the pitch.

I was making progress. My football intelligence was improving and my body was also starting to fill out. There was a big gym culture at Ipswich and I was on the weights a lot, honing my physique and preparing for the challenges ahead by finally putting some muscle on my skinny frame.

Not that it was all plain sailing. There was a sharp edge to Jim, whose inexperience didn't stop him telling it like it is, and I discovered that he wasn't to be crossed when I took him on during a 1–0 defeat away to Colchester United.

Maybe he thought I needed to be taken down a peg or two. I wasn't happy about Jim starting Sylvain Legwinski and Simon Walton in central midfield and sticking me on the left wing. I kept drifting inside during the first half and I wasn't prepared to listen to Jim, who was screaming at me to move back to the left. 'I'm not getting the ball,' I shouted. 'Put me in centre midfield.'

Big mistake. Jim tore into me in the dressing room at half-time. 'You f**king little prick,' he said, standing about a centimetre away from my face. 'You ever tell me to f**king put you in centre midfield again, I'll put you in the stand. Who the f**k do you think you are – Rivellino?'

I didn't dare answer back. I was wrong to challenge the manager's authority, although Jim didn't hold it against me. When I arrived for training in the morning he got me in a headlock and laughed. 'Hey,' he said, 'what about last night?'

It was water under the bridge as far as he was concerned. He kept picking me and I could feel the confidence flowing back into my game. The change of scenery had given me a new lease of life. I felt like a man and I was ready to go back to West Ham when my three months at Ipswich were up. My mind was made up. West Ham were in a relegation battle after making a dreadful start to the season and I didn't want to watch them suffer from afar any more. It was time to go home.

* * *

I had big ambitions after playing my final game for Ipswich, a 2–0 defeat to Sheffield Wednesday at the start of November. West Ham had changed while I was away. It was astonishing when they shocked the football world by signing two Argentinian internationals on the final day of the summer transfer window. Nobody knew how they had pulled it off, and I was staggered when I wandered into the canteen at Ipswich's training ground, looked at the TV and saw the news about Carlos Tevez and Javier Mascherano joining West Ham. 'Bloody hell,' I thought. 'What's gone on now?'

It made no sense. 'Come on, how have you signed those two?' the boys at Ipswich said. 'You've got no chance of going back now. Mascherano's going to take your position. You might as well stay here with us.'

Strangely, though, the signings of Tevez and Mascherano didn't help West Ham. They both found it difficult to settle in England and their arrivals put a few noses out of joint. Some players were worried about losing their places, even though the standard of training was higher, and the team began to struggle, crashing out of the UEFA Cup after a heavy defeat to Palermo in the first round.

It was a reality check. There was so much optimism after our run to the FA Cup final, but the Premier League is an unforgiving place. Once the rut set in it was hard for Pards to steer the lads back onto the right path, restore their confidence and guide them away from danger.

Had the magic dried up? At times it seemed we were cursed. It felt like a bad omen when Dean Ashton, our first-choice striker, went on England duty just before our opening league game and was ruled out for the season after breaking his ankle in training. Nothing went right. I watched from afar as results deteriorated and, given that it was only our second season in the top flight, the media inevitably began to write stories about an undisciplined dressing room.

Was it complacency? A lack of focus? It's hard for me to say as I was at Ipswich when things started to go wrong, although some of my old team-mates have since said they were guilty of believing their own hype and taking their eye off the ball.

In their defence they weren't working in an easy atmosphere. It was a strange time for the club. Terry Brown, the chairman, was about to sell it to a consortium led by the Icelandic billionaire Björgólfur Guðmundsson, and Carlos and Javier weren't living up to expectations. 'I can play in this team,' I thought. 'If I go back and help us stay up, it's going to be amazing.'

But Pards had other ideas when my time at Ipswich was over. I was hurt and disappointed when he said that I needed to go out on another loan. It angered me when we sold Chris Cohen to Yeovil for £70,000, which was an absolute steal for a player of his quality, and I was worried that Pards was trying to get me out of the club too.

I had to stand my ground. Another young player might have decided to leave but I was never going to give up on a career at West Ham. 'No,' I said. 'I don't want to go away again. I'm ready and I'm good enough to play for you.'

There was no need to panic. I knew there was a chance that Pards was going to be fired soon and I didn't want to be out on loan when a new manager arrived. I could see that Javier was struggling to adapt to the pace of English football. He was at fault for a goal when we lost at Everton at the start of December and the pressure on Pards was immense after we lost at home to Wigan.

Nothing was working. Carlos was trying hard and had our support, but he didn't speak English and was frustrated with how it was going on the pitch. He kept missing chances and he landed himself in hot water when he reacted badly to Pards substituting him during a home win over Sheffield United at the end of November. It wasn't on, and the situation became more awkward when we said that Carlos, who was ordered to donate some of his wages to charity, also had to train in a Brazil shirt for two weeks after Pards tried to lighten the atmosphere by letting us decide on our Argentinian superstar's punishment.

It didn't go down well with Carlos. Pards tried to convince him but he was fighting a losing battle. Carlos was never going to back down. 'If you make me wear a Brazil shirt then you won't ever see me play for West Ham again,' he said through his interpreter.

We needed a new approach. Pards was clinging on to his job and I wanted to help, but he never gave me a chance. Three days after losing to Wigan we went up to Bolton and I was disappointed to see Christian Dailly, who was a centre-back, starting in midfield. It was a disaster. Carlos looked lost on the right wing and it was over for Pards after Bolton smashed us 4–0. The club were left with no choice.

*   *   *

We needed a saviour. Alan Curbishley, who was available after leaving Charlton Athletic, fitted the bill. Curbs was an East End lad, a former West Ham player and had done a brilliant job at Charlton. His appointment gave me a new lease of life. Curbs was a hugely experienced manager and, although he left me out at first, it seemed the board had made the right choice when we beat Manchester United at Upton Park in his opening game.

Yet our problems went deeper than Curbs realised. We stumbled through our next three games and tempers boiled over when we visited newly promoted Reading on New Year's Day. I was next to Teddy Sheringham in the stands and couldn't believe what I was watching as Reading beat us 6–0.

The backlash was huge. The supporters were raging and there were more stories in the press about the side's poor attitude. Curbs was fuming. He didn't hold back during his press conference after the Reading game, bemoaning the culture in the dressing room and criticising players who seemed more interested in buying Baby Bentleys than wearing the badge with pride.

The Baby Bentleys line inevitably grabbed the headlines. It was an eye-catching quote from Curbs, and to outsiders it must have seemed like a plausible explanation for West Ham's rapid descent into chaos. Truthfully, though, sometimes the reality in football is more mundane. We had young players like Bobby Zamora, Marlon Harewood, Anton Ferdinand and Nigel Reo-Coker. They were brilliant during our run to the cup final and nobody was worrying about them having nice cars when everything was going well on the pitch. Football can be a fickle game. Something that seems harmless can suddenly become unacceptable.

Nigel seemed to suffer more than most. He was a terrific athlete and a good midfielder, but he was our captain and the fans expected him to lift the team when times were tough. It was wrong to heap so much responsibility on a young player's shoulders. There was a lot of pressure on Nigel, who was still learning about the game, and I think that it weighed him down and had a negative impact on his performances, which made the fans think that he wasn't trying hard enough.

It was clear that something had to change. Curbs wasn't prepared to take any nonsense and he began to look for people who could give the team a fresher feel. We needed some new faces and I was eager to impress when I finally came into the side against Brighton at home in the third round of the FA Cup.

'I'm not letting go of my place now,' I thought as I jumped into Teddy's outstretched arms after giving us the lead with a sharp volley early in the second half. It was my first goal for the club and it felt like I had finally arrived. 'This is where I want to be,' I thought. 'I wasn't ready before, but it's going to be different this time.'

But Curbs was about to burst my bubble. I didn't play again for ages after the win over Brighton and I had a battle on my hands after the owners gave Curbs a big budget for new signings. Nigel Quashie, an experienced midfielder, came in, and we were linked with a host of names throughout the month. It was hard to keep up at times. Javier left to join Liverpool and Ashley Young turned us down to join Aston Villa, but Curbs still managed to strengthen the squad before the window shut.

Luís Boa Morte, a £5.5m signing from Fulham, was a strong guy and had a good left foot. Matthew Upson and Calum Davenport improved our options in central defence. And Lucas Neill, a target for Liverpool, instantly lifted the mood when he signed from Blackburn.

I loved playing with Lucas, who was a classy right-back, an experienced professional and a top leader. He was a great influence on me and the team. Suddenly, after so much doom and gloom, it seemed we had a chance of saving ourselves.

But the clock was ticking. Charlton, Sheffield United, Watford and Wigan were also fighting hard to stay up, and we were running out of chances. We went ages without winning in the league after beating United in Curbs's first game, and we were under huge pressure when we visited Charlton at the end of February.

I had done my best to convince Curbs to play me. I kept going to his office to wear him down, but he was stubborn. 'Don't worry,' he said. 'You'll get your chance.'

It was supposed to come against Charlton. I was going to be in the team before Kepa Blanco, a Spanish striker on loan from Sevilla, caught me with a bad tackle in training. My ankle blew up, although it was a blessing in disguise. The game was a disaster. Pards had just taken over at Charlton and he was understandably delighted after thrashing us 4–0.

I was relieved not to have played. I focused on getting fit – I spent the rest of the weekend with my foot in a bucket of ice – and made a quick return to training. Our next game was Spurs at home, and Kevin Keen, who coached me in the academy, said he was going to push Curbs to pick me. I was training well and Curbs didn't take much convincing. 'You're going to play against Spurs,' he said. 'Make sure you're ready.'

I wasn't short of motivation. There was a different feel to us. Carlos was in the zone and we were on the same wavelength. We had a connection on the pitch, even though he barely spoke any English, and he set me up when I gave us an early lead, chesting the ball down for me to ping a low shot past Paul Robinson from the edge of the area.

It was an incredible moment. The noise from the crowd was on another level to when I scored against Brighton, and the volume grew even louder when Carlos finally ended his wait for a goal in claret and blue, doubling our lead with a curling free-kick just before half-time. The fans loved it. They adored Carlos, who always gave his all, and embraced him like one of their own when he jumped into the crowd to celebrate his goal.

Upton Park was rocking but Spurs came back in the second half. They made it 2–2 and refused to lie down when Carlos swung in a free-kick for Bobby Zamora to restore our lead. I was devastated when they scored two late goals to win 4–3. I couldn't stop myself from crying my eyes out on the pitch. The emotions were raw. It was such a cruel way to lose and I couldn't hide my pain.

There were nine games left and it felt like we were down. As the disappointment faded, though, we began to focus on the positives. The Spurs game was a turning point. We gained some self-belief from playing so well against a very good side and took the first steps towards survival when we travelled to Blackburn Rovers a week later, battling back from 1–0 down and earning three crucial points thanks to a winning goal that was allowed to stand despite the ball not crossing the line.

Was the great escape on? Carlos's improvement gave us hope. He scored our equaliser against Blackburn and was developing a connection with Bobby. We had hope. The defence was improving and I felt like a proper player at last. I was in my element when we hosted Middlesbrough at the end of March. They had a Brazilian midfielder, Fábio Rochemback, and I hit him with a few strong tackles early on. I could tell he didn't fancy it. I flew into him when the ball ran to him in Middlesbrough's half, the ball broke to Carlos and he crossed for Bobby to give us the lead.

Carlos tore them apart. He made it 2–0 before half-time and in the second half I watched in awe as he produced one piece of skill on Middlesbrough's left-back, Emanuel

Pogatetz, that should have been illegal. I'd never seen anything like it before – but that was Carlos. He was feeling the love from the fans and was finally showing why he was regarded as one of the best strikers in the world.

*   *   *

It wasn't just about Carlos. As a team we felt unbeatable. Yossi Benayoun perked up. Nigel found some form. Lucas was immense at right-back. Robert Green made a series of astonishing saves when we visited Arsenal at the start of April. The pressure was relentless from the first whistle, but nothing got past Greeno. We were defiant. After a few minutes I followed Gilberto Silva into the corner and hit him with a thunderous tackle in front of the West Ham fans, who greeted the challenge with a huge roar.

Admittedly we had a lot of luck. Arsenal missed so many chances after Bobby gave us a shock lead just before half-time. Somehow we survived and held on for a huge win. 'We can stay up now,' I thought. 'We've got a chance.'

There was still a lot to do after our win over Arsenal. We hadn't clawed our way out of the bottom three and there wasn't much goodwill coming our way. The other teams scrapping for survival weren't happy about how we had signed Carlos and Javier. There were questions about third-party ownership from the Premier League, who opened an investigation into the transfers, and the atmosphere was spiky when we visited Sheffield United. They were above us and we were back in trouble after losing 3–0.

It was a horrible day. They loved beating us because of the controversy over Carlos, and the defeat brought us crashing back down to earth. We realised that going on a decent run had made us take our eye off the ball and it was lucky that we had some good senior professionals in the dressing room. We had to get back to basics. There was no room for any complacency.

Yet our situation didn't look any better when we lost 4–1 at home to Chelsea in our next game. The only highlight was Carlos cutting inside from the left and making it 1–1 with a brilliant long-range shot. The noise was deafening when he scored, but Chelsea quickly took control again. They were far too strong and I lost my rag in the second half, shushing José Mourinho when he shouted at me for making a bad tackle on one of his players.

I couldn't help myself in the heat of the moment. José came on the pitch at full-time and I went over to apologise to him. 'José, it was in the middle of the game,' I said. 'I didn't mean to be disrespectful.'

But José wasn't bothered. 'F**k off, I loved it,' he said. 'Listen, I've watched you over the last couple of months. You've been fantastic and keep up the good work – you're a top, top player.'

I was speechless. José's praise gave me such a huge boost and I was determined not to give up. We still had time to save ourselves and our optimism returned after a brilliant goal from Bobby earned us a 1–0 win over Everton in our next game.

The Great Escape was back on and we felt confident before travelling to Wigan for a must-win game. Away from the pitch, though, the allegations about the club breaking third-party ownership rules when Carlos and Javier arrived were only growing louder. There was talk of us being hit with a points deduction, which would have made relegation a certainty, and at times it seemed that we were the most unpopular team in the country.

But I wasn't bothered about the criticism from outside – footballers don't really pay much attention to that kind of thing. The situation was out of our control and it made no difference to our preparations when the Premier League fined the club £5.5m a day before the Wigan game. I didn't care. From my perspective the punishment would have been more severe if the club had really stepped out of line. They'd have banned Carlos if we'd done something really serious. But there was no points deduction, despite the complaints from our rivals, and the fine looked like a price worth paying once it was confirmed that Carlos was going to be available for the rest of the season.

We needed him. Carlos had come into his own and I was full of adrenaline. I wasn't thinking about third-party ownership. My sole focus was on survival. I was desperate to save West Ham, and make my family and friends happy. My loans at Hull and Ipswich were in the past, and I was finally showing that I was capable of playing in the Premier League every week. 'I'm going to prove everyone wrong if we stay up,' I thought. 'They'll know that West Ham is where I belong.'

I had never felt so determined. I loved Pards but I hadn't forgotten about him trying to send me out on loan again. It spurred me on and part of me thought that I would be a hero if I could help West Ham avoid relegation.

Yet I didn't have to do it on my own. Everyone played well when we beat Wigan 3–0. Carlos was outstanding, Yossi was instrumental in virtually everything good on the pitch, and Luís Boa Morte, who opened the scoring with a clever lob, taught me a valuable lesson when he played an unselfish pass for Marlon Harewood to score our third goal.

It was a sign that our unity had finally returned. Marlon was a cracking player but he had gone ages without a goal. He needed someone to show him some kindness, and Boa knew that helping out a team-mate who was low on confidence was more important than going for personal glory. 'It isn't about individuals,' I thought as I watched Marlon thank Boa. 'It's about the team.'

That goal meant so much to Marlon. Fans don't know what players go through in private. They can only judge from what they see on the pitch. They don't know what we're like as people, so if I ever heard my mates from home criticising a West Ham player I would always try to give them a different perspective. 'Wait a minute,' I'd say. 'You don't even know them. I'd like to think you'd defend me if you heard someone slagging me off.'

Boa is a good example. He wasn't particularly popular with the crowd but I think he was great. He was a proper team player and he made another strong contribution when we followed up our win over Wigan by beating Bolton at Upton Park in our penultimate game. We were unplayable. Carlos gave us an early lead with a superb free-kick and he scored again after I combined with Boa on the left.

Bolton couldn't live with the speed and quality of our football. Carlos was in his element and I could feel my game improving because of him. I was ready to try things, and we were 3–0 up after half an hour, Carlos crossing for me to smash an unstoppable volley past Jussi Jääskeläinen.

I was buzzing after the game, as we were finally out of the relegation zone after holding on for a 3–1 win. I was still thinking about my goal when Teddy Sheringham came up to me in the dressing room. 'Well played, son,' he said. 'Talk to me about the volley. What was going on in your head when the ball was coming over?'

'To be honest, mate, just hit it as sweet as I can,' I said. 'And obviously use the pace of the ball to beat the keeper. That's all that mattered.'

But that wasn't good enough for Teddy. 'What?' he said. 'You didn't think about what part of the goal to put it in? What part of the boot to hit it with? Whether to hit the ball low so the keeper had less chance of saving it?'

It stopped me in my tracks. 'That's why he played at the highest level and scored so many goals,' I thought while I was driving home. 'It's because of his brain. I just tried to hit it as hard as possible.'

Teddy had forced me into a reassessment. When Carlos crossed I was already getting ready to celebrate. 'This is perfect,' I thought as the ball fell on to my right foot, 'this is going to be unreal.' But that was naive. Teddy would have been far more analytical, and his advice made me think more about my game. I needed to be more clinical. I thought about Teddy and considered why he would pop the ball up for me when we did shooting drills in training. It wasn't random; it was because it was easier to hit the ball when it was off the floor.

That was Teddy: always one step ahead. I never played with anyone more intelligent than him. Teddy was always thinking about how to make his team-mates better and he had a huge influence on my career. When I looked at him I realised that I still had so much to learn.

* * *

I was building up momentum but there was no guarantee that I was going to be a Premier League player when the season was over. Everything depended on whether we could nick a result against Manchester United on the final day. Watford and Charlton were already down but Sheffield United and Wigan still had a chance of staying up, and although our fate was in our hands, we could not have asked for a tougher assignment than a trip to Old Trafford.

It was still too close to call. We were in 17th place, below Sheffield United on goal difference, and Wigan were three points below us. We still needed a point to be sure of staying up and, to add to the sense of drama, Sheffield United were hosting Wigan at Bramall Lane. We could take nothing for granted and I was already jittery when I woke up on the morning of the game. 'Please, God, let us win,' I thought.

I knew that we were up against it. United had already won the league and had a brilliant home record, though the one saving grace was that they were about to face Chelsea in the FA Cup final. It meant that Sir Alex

Ferguson decided to rest a few players, which increased our chances of causing an upset.

We felt confident and the journey to the ground was good. I sat at the back of the coach with our big red-haired centre-back James Collins, and he helped me relax by saying that we were going to win. I needed to hear that from Ginge. It made me think that we were going to do it. There was no panic. The dressing room was calm and we managed to hold our own during the early stages, even though Sir Alex had clearly sent them out to win. Michael Carrick and Wayne Rooney were playing, and we rode our luck at times. Yossi had to clear a shot off the line, and although we spent much of the first half defending, it felt like destiny when Carlos stirred on the stroke of half-time, linking up with Bobby before charging through the United defence to give us a shock lead.

The goal gave us breathing space. Wigan were beating Sheffield United, who were going down, and United flew at us in the second half. It was relentless, and the pressure increased when Sir Alex brought Ryan Giggs, Paul Scholes and Cristiano Ronaldo off the bench after an hour. My heart sank when I saw those three coming on – but we kept repelling United's attacks. 'F**k me, Nobes,' Ginge said with 15 minutes left. 'I think we're going to do it.'

It was pure relief when the final whistle blew. People had written us off but we were safe. It was an incredible feeling, and I was emotional when I went to celebrate with the fans. Dad was in the crowd and my mates were there too. As a homegrown lad, it was overwhelming for me to think that I had come out of nowhere to help my team stay in the Premier League.

I finally felt like I belonged on that stage. I had grown up. I had frozen 18 months earlier, chasing shadows when Pards put me up against Scholes at Upton Park, but I was a different player now. 'I deserve to be here,' I thought when we walked out at Old Trafford. 'I've earned this.'

I was excited. We travelled back to London to celebrate and people kept sending me messages of congratulation. I loved the adulation, and my performances meant that my agent, Dave Geiss, was able to talk to the club about rewarding me with a new contract. I went to Cyprus with Carly and told her about the club offering me the kind of money I never thought I'd earn. Both of us were blown away. We were only kids and had never seen numbers like that before.

Yet while it was clear that the club valued me, I soon began to fret about my place. I found it hard to not to doubt myself. Our Icelandic owners were planning to invest in the squad during the summer and I was worried about my place when I read about the players we wanted to sign. What did it mean for me? Was I going to be sent out on loan again? It wasn't much of a holiday in the end.

I couldn't relax. 'I can't wait to get back,' I thought. 'I can't be on the bench again. As soon as I get back in pre-season I'm going to go to Curbs's office and tell him that I want to be in his team. I can't stop now. I want to be the number one.'

4

Mental Strain

The feelings of insecurity lingered for much of the summer. Curbs had money to spend and my fears about my position increased when we strengthened in central midfield by signing Scott Parker from Newcastle. Scott was an England international and his arrival made me think that I was going to lose my place in the starting 11. Change was in the air. For Curbs, this was a golden chance to alter the make-up of his squad. There was a sense of him trying to start afresh. Nigel Reo-Coker and Marlon Harewood being sold to Aston Villa felt like a sign of where things were heading, and although Curbs would have preferred not to have lost Carlos Tevez to Manchester United and Yossi Benayoun to Liverpool, the board did not restrict him from bringing in new players.

The big signings did not finish with Scott. We paid a lot of money to sign the French winger Julien Faubert from Bordeaux. Freddie Ljungberg, who was one of the best attackers in the league, joined on high wages after leaving Arsenal on a free transfer. We replaced Carlos by buying Craig Bellamy from Liverpool and were trying to bolster our midfield further by signing Kieron Dyer from Newcastle.

Yet I couldn't stop worrying about my future. The fact that I was moving in the right direction didn't improve my mood as the reality of the situation wasn't lost on me. I came back from my holiday with Carly and immediately went off to a short training camp with the England Under-21s in Valencia, where I did enough to convince Stuart Pearce to name me in his squad for that summer's European Under-21 Championship in the Netherlands. Anton Ferdinand and Nigel Reo-Coker were also involved, which meant there were a couple of familiar faces, and the tournament went well for me. We had some good players and while I began our first game against the Czech Republic on the bench, I managed to be named in the starting 11 after replacing Tom Huddlestone when we played Italy in the following game.

I had a great time. We made it out of a difficult group and our semi-final against the Netherlands was unforgettable. They denied us victory with a last-minute equaliser and there was barely anything between us during a marathon penalty shootout. I scored twice from the spot and we gave everything to reach the final, but it wasn't meant to be. The Netherlands went through, winning the shootout 13–12, and I was so heartbroken that I ended up crying on the pitch again.

Nonetheless it was still an achievement to reach the last four. We could be proud of our efforts and I realised how much coverage the tournament had received when I went on holiday with Carly again. People kept coming up to me to talk about it. 'Great tournament, Mark,' they'd say. 'You didn't deserve to lose that game.'

It was good to hear. And yet I still couldn't stop thinking about going back to West Ham for pre-season and finding that I wasn't in Curbs's plans. That nagging feeling in the back of my mind wouldn't go away but I was good at keeping my emotions hidden from the people around me. I didn't talk to anyone about my concerns – not even Carly – as I didn't want anyone to think I was weak. My anxiety about missing out stopped me from saying yes when Curbs offered me an extra week off, even though it would have benefited me physically to have more time to recover from playing for England.

I put it down to inexperience. I wanted to make it seem like I didn't care, even though I did. I was busy negotiating a new contract and I didn't want to make Carly worry. It was silly. I should have found a way to get things off my chest but I was too young to realise that it wasn't healthy to keep things bottled up.

Unfortunately football still needs to become more accepting when it comes to mental health. It's such a physical sport, so if you go in and say that your hamstring's feeling sore then you're given a scan to see if you need to stop training. But if you say that you're not feeling good mentally then it's more frowned upon. It isn't treated like an injury.

The sport should be more open. I was only 20 years old but people don't look at you as a kid when you've been out on loan, forced your way into the West Ham team and are starting to earn good money. It is tough, and some people struggle to handle the mental pressure of having to perform week in, week out. It's easy to fall by the wayside if you don't have the right support.

Part of the problem is that footballers worry about being judged if they say they're having a hard time. They're scared of expressing their true emotions in case people accuse them of whining. You have to be so careful with what you say in public. The money at the top level is huge, so when normal people are struggling to put food on the table it's easy for them to fall into the trap of thinking that footballers who go through issues with their mental health are spoilt and ungrateful.

It's too easy to look at the world that way. A lot of footballers come from working-class backgrounds and know what it's like to have nothing. At the end of the day we're all human. Some of the best players in the world have struggled with the mental side of the game. It can happen to anyone – and although the situation has improved in recent years, footballers still need to be encouraged to talk more.

I didn't speak to anyone when my parents got divorced and Dad moved into my flat in Gidea Park. It affected me but I kept it to myself. I cared because I'd had a happy childhood and didn't want our family dynamic to change, but where was I supposed to take those feelings? Football was my emotional release and I was lucky that I had West Ham as a distraction, which is why I never wanted to abandon them when things were difficult on the pitch.

Even then, though, I never had many real conversations with my team-mates. I loved the dressing-room banter, but it was a macho environment. It's interesting that players speak more openly after retiring. I look at Craig Bellamy, who never held back with his opinions during his career, saying after hanging up his boots that he'd had mental health problems while in the game. People hide it away. I could always tell that Kieron Dyer was carrying a lot of anger around, but I never knew he took his emotions out on other people. I was so proud of him when he explained that his pain came from being sexually abused as a child. I just wish that I'd known about it when we were team-mates.

It's why I try to treat everyone the same way. You never know if people are going through something behind closed doors. I certainly wasn't adept at processing my emotions when I was younger. Maybe it's why the tears always came out on the pitch.

*   *   *

Having the right mentality is vital if you want to succeed at the highest level. I had to be ready to fight for my place. I couldn't let suggestions that Kieron was close to completing his move from Newcastle throw me off course. There was plenty of competition in midfield – Scott, Lee Bowyer and Hayden Mullins were all more experienced than me – and I couldn't give Curbs any reason to leave me out when we hosted Manchester City on the opening day of the 2007–08 season.

I trained hard and was in the team against City – but the game didn't go well. They had just hired Sven-Göran Eriksson and had spent big on a few foreign players. Elano, their clever Brazilian midfielder, ran the show. I couldn't get close to him and the mood was flat after we lost 2–0, with our supporters worried that it was going to be another difficult season.

The defeat was a wake-up call. We had to improve when we visited Birmingham City in our second game. I was growing out of being the young, local lad and had to take on greater responsibility as more was expected of me. I had a good relationship with Curbs, who had placed a lot of trust in me, and I needed to make sure that I paid him back.

Shrinking back into my shell wasn't an option. I didn't mind the pressure; I thrived on it. I knew that I had to step up and I was ready when my chance arrived against Birmingham. It was a tight game, and it looked like it was going to finish 0–0 until Craig Bellamy went through on goal midway through the second half and won us a penalty after being fouled by the keeper.

I didn't hesitate when the referee pointed to the spot. Bellers was a senior player but I decided to chance my arm. I ran to pick up the ball, assuming that someone would take it off me. Nobody reacted, though. The penalty was mine. It was my first for West Ham and I wasn't scared. I earned us the points by sending the keeper the wrong way, celebrated by sliding in front of our supporters and realised that I wanted to feel that buzz again.

The mind works in funny ways. I always felt confident before taking a penalty. The goal never looked smaller to me. 'I'll be a hero when I score,' I thought. The possibility that I might miss never fazed me. Weirdly, I only felt nervous after scoring. I couldn't stop myself from worrying about what would have happened if I'd missed.

Fortunately I didn't miss many during my career. I scored 38 out of my 43 penalties for West Ham, and I followed up my effort against Birmingham by scoring from the spot when we beat Liverpool at Upton Park a few months later. Now this was pressure. Liverpool were a very good side and we were on our way to picking up a decent point when one last counterattack ended with Jamie Carragher catching Freddie Ljungberg in the area in the final minute. 'This is what I've been waiting for,' I thought as I grabbed the ball and walked towards the spot. 'My chance to score one at home.'

I didn't give a second's thought about Liverpool's goal-keeper, Pepe Reina, having a history of saving penalties. I trusted myself. 'This is going to be unreal,' I thought. There was no doubt in my mind. I opened up my body, stayed calm and made my choice: inside of the right foot, low to the keeper's left. It was a huge moment and I was delighted when the ball went past Reina, who couldn't get there in time despite correctly guessing which side I'd picked.

Accuracy was key. Reina's anticipation was good and he went the right way again when I scored from the spot against Liverpool in 2012. 'I'm going to save one of your penalties one day,' he told me after the game. It was probably for the best that I never took another one against him.

My first ever Sunday League team, Barking Colts, alongside the legend that is Sir Trevor Brooking.

With Alan Brazil at Heath Park & Redbridge – winning player of the year.

Having a kickabout in the garden with my friends James and Billy Short.

Enjoying some downtime with some of my England Under-17s team-mates.

Meeting Prince Harry with
Anton Ferdinand.

Battling with Carl Cort on my league
debut for West Ham against Wolves,
January 2005.

Carlos Tevez scored a brace in our 3–1
defeat of Bolton in May 2007, finally taking
us out of the relegation zone.

Celebrating my first goal for the club,
in a third-round FA Cup game against
Brighton, 2007.

Taking on Blackburn Rovers at Ewood Park, 2009. It was my 100th game for the Hammers and I marked the occasion by scoring the opening goal.

Our 3–2 loss to Wigan in May 2011 saw us relegated from the Premier League for the first – and only – time in my career.

Up against Moussa Sissoko in November 2014, during my 205th appearance in the Premier League, a club record.

With my son Lenny at my testimonial, March 2016.

Farewell to the Boleyn, May 2016. Our last match at the ground
was a 3–2 win against Manchester United.

My 300th Premier League appearance in December 2017, which I marked by rifling one in from the penalty spot against Stoke.

Celebrating scoring the second goal in our 2–0 defeat of Leicester at the King Power Stadium, May 2018.

I loved European nights. We drew Lyon in the last eight of the Europa Cup in 2022, beating them over two legs to reach our first major European semi-final in 46 years.

I can't hold back the tears at my final home game in a
West Ham shirt, London Stadium, May 2022.

Of course, I'd have backed myself to get the better of Reina if we'd faced each other for a third time. I never worried about goalkeepers. If you take penalties all the time you're bound to miss a few eventually. It's inevitable. The question is whether you're capable of handling the disappointment. I experienced failure from the spot for the first time when I was denied by Hull City's Matt Duke in January 2009, but it didn't put me off. I wanted the ball when we won a penalty against Chelsea a few months later. We were losing 1–0 and Petr Čech, Chelsea's goalkeeper, didn't intimidate me. Funnily enough our former goal-keeping coach, Ludo Mikloško, had invited Čech to our training ground to help us practise taking penalties before the play-off final against Preston in 2005. I didn't miss once.

This time, though, Čech got the better of me. The points were on the line and he read my mind, diving to his left to push the ball away. I was gutted, but it was all part of the learning process. We lost 1–0 and Frank Lampard walked over at full-time, put his arm around me and offered me some precious advice. 'Make sure you take the next one,' Frank said. 'And make sure you smash it in the back of the net.'

* * *

Frank was spot on. I hit my next penalty like I was Julian Dicks, walloping the ball into the top corner when we beat Aston Villa in November 2009. It was a break from my usual routine. My preferred style was to minimise the risk. Over time I developed a technique that allowed me to take the goalkeeper out of the game more often than not. I was careful. Goalkeepers are clever. They watch everything you do, so you have to mix it up. I made sure that I kept them guessing and I realised my chances of scoring increased if I watched which way the goalkeeper was going. I only needed a little look before I hit the ball. It all happened in a split second and if I judged it correctly then I was able to play it safe. I didn't have to put the ball in the corner if the keeper went the wrong way; I just had to make sure that it was on target. If you look closely you'll see that a lot of my penalties were aimed quite close to the middle of the goal.

That method served me well. I always tried to watch the keeper's movement and if I saw him going the right way I'd usually respond by lifting the ball a little higher. It was all about concentration. Penalties often made the difference between success and failure, and the only time I ever I took my eye off the ball was when we played Spurs at home on the opening day of the 2013–14 season. I got cocky. It was 0–0, I saw Hugo Lloris go the wrong way and I got ahead of myself. 'I've done it,' I thought. 'I've scored.

It's too easy.' Big mistake. I was already celebrating but I wasn't thinking clearly. I aimed for the side netting corner, which was unnecessary, and watched in horror when the ball dribbled wide.

I was kicking myself, especially as we ended up losing the game in the last minute. It was the only time I ever missed the target, the only time I ever lost my focus. I made sure that it never happened again. It's different if a keeper makes a save. That usually happened if I didn't see him move in time, but I could live with that. It happens.

At the end of the day it's just a penalty. I never bothered practising them. I didn't want the lads watching me. It's never nice to miss a penalty, even in training, and I always preferred to have that bad feeling when it really mattered. I didn't see any value in taking a penalty in a non-pressurised situation. I didn't even like taking them in pre-season. 'What's the point when it doesn't really matter?' I thought. 'I'd rather save myself for the real thing.'

Penalties were my forte. I didn't worry about my lack of goals from open play. I was never like Lampard or Gerrard. I was more suited to being behind the play. I enjoyed sitting back, dictating, knitting moves together, and never tried to be someone else.

I only scored once from open play during the 2007–08 season. We played Newcastle at home at the end of April and I decided to gamble early on, breaking into the box and using my left foot to sweep a cross from our left-back, George McCartney, past Steve Harper.

It was a nice finish and I immediately ran over to George to thank him for the assist. He was a quiet lad but we were really good mates. We liked to get to training early to play intense games of football golf with some of the coaches and it seemed that nothing could keep us apart – until we suddenly found ourselves at each other's throats during a training session one afternoon, that is.

We both completely lost our heads. It was a silly argument, a row over who was meant to be tracking a runner, and before I knew it we were swinging punches at each other. The other lads didn't know what to make of it. 'What are you two doing?' they said. 'You're best mates! Why are you fighting?'

That's football for you. I never saw the row coming and we were friends again after training. Curbs hauled us into his office and I made it clear that I wasn't going to hold a grudge against George. We laughed about it when I scored against Newcastle. There were no problems in the dressing room and the season passed by without anything particularly dramatic happening. Only injuries to key players held us back. We cruised along in mid-table for much of the campaign, never in danger of being sucked into trouble, never likely to challenge for a European place, and were satisfied to finish 10th.

*   *   *

We fancied ourselves to improve if we could keep more of our players fit. It seemed that we were building. The board had invested, we had a solid British core and we had talent in key positions. Bellers was a top player. He was always playing off the shoulder of the last defender and I loved being able to hit balls over the top for him to chase.

But the summer was weird. It gradually became apparent that the club was in financial trouble. The board had handed out too many big contracts, the recession was starting and the Icelandic economy had collapsed. The banks were going crazy. Eggert Magnússon, the chairman, was doing his best to keep spirits high, and the mood was fine when he invited us to his Canary Wharf flat for a barbecue during pre-season. But the situation away from the pitch was deteriorating and Curbs didn't have much money to spend. Instead it was all about cutting costs. Freddie Ljungberg left on a free transfer, and it didn't feel particularly encouraging when we trimmed our squad by selling Bobby Zamora and John Paintsil before the start of the 2008–09 season.

The atmosphere was uncertain. We started the season by beating Wigan at home, but I didn't play well and Curbs pulled me into his office after the weekend. 'What's wrong?' he said. 'What happened? I didn't see that aggression from you.' I didn't have an answer. I was off the pace and I let the team down when we lost 3–0 to Manchester City in our second game, leaving the boys in the lurch by getting sent off for two silly bookings in the first half.

We were well beaten and the negativity deepened when we sold Anton Ferdinand to Sunderland shortly before the end of the transfer window. Curbs wasn't impressed. He sought assurances that no more players would leave but his patience was wearing thin. The joy of beating Blackburn 4–1 at the end of August did not last long. The decision to sell George McCartney to Sunderland just before the window shut was the final straw. Curbs couldn't take any more. He quit, accusing the board of breaching his trust, and we found ourselves in a strange position: managerless after picking up six points from our first three games.

The dressing room was shocked. I got on with Curbs and wasn't aware of his frustrations. As players we had no insight into the board's decisions. We had to get on with it and we were intrigued when Gianfranco Zola was appointed as our new manager.

It was a big call to choose Gianfranco given that it was his first job in management. We wanted to make life easier for him. Gianfranco was such a nice guy and we all remembered the wonderful goals he scored for Chelsea. His playing career inspired respect and it was clear that he hadn't lost any of his ability when he joined in with us at training. Gianfranco was still incredibly fit, he still knew how to whip a free-kick into the top corner and he did a lot of work with me on an individual basis after training.

I was enthralled by Gianfranco's footballing philosophy. He wanted to introduce a more expansive style and his first training session was so sharp. Gianfranco was inexperienced, so it was a wise move to bring in Steve Clarke as his assistant. Steve had worked for José Mourinho at Chelsea and he was incredibly detailed. Everything was structured, and the likes of Bellers, Matthew Upson, Scott Parker and Lee Bowyer were excited by the increased tempo.

I connected with Gianfranco. He introduced me to yoga and we spoke a lot about football. I could tell that he rated me. He saw my football brain. He gave me freedom to express myself on the pitch and I got an assist for our new Italian striker, David Di Michele, when we beat Newcastle 3–1 in Gianfranco's first game. 'I think this could be really enjoyable,' Scott Parker said. 'We passed the ball so well.'

Yet it wasn't plain sailing all the way. We had a wobble before Christmas and I was injured for a while. I wasn't having a good time. I struggled after regaining fitness, got taken off during a win over Portsmouth on Boxing Day and found myself having a difficult conversation with Gianfranco at training. 'Look, I'm not going to play you this weekend,' he said. 'You need a rest.'

I looked in Gianfranco's eyes and could see that he was as upset as me. He didn't want to drop me but I hadn't given him much of a choice. I needed a kick up the arse and I was determined not to let him down when I won my place back. That was the thing about Gianfranco: you wanted to play for him. Players wanted to do well for him. A few weeks later we went to Newcastle and drew 2–2 after I missed a chance to kill them off, but Gianfranco didn't tear into me. He sat next to me in the dressing room, patted my head and said, 'You owe me one.'

Those words stayed with me. I kept plugging away and got my reward during a 1–1 draw with Blackburn. It was a really good goal, a clever effort with the outside of my right foot, and my main thought was that I had finally paid Gianfranco back.

He gave me confidence. He wanted us to take risks on the ball and we began to play some excellent football. We were fearless. We were unfortunate only to draw with Chelsea at Stamford Bridge and we gave teams problems with our midfield diamond. I picked passes, Valon Behrami ran all day and Scott Parker made sure that we were never without the ball for long.

I learnt a lot from Scotty. He taught me not to dwell on the ball in training, rattling into me if I kept hold of possession too long. I was lucky to have leaders like him, Matty Upson and Lucas Neill around. I still have a good relationship with Scotty. We spoke the same football language and the fans loved his all-action tackling, although he was far more technically gifted than many people realised.

You could always count on Scotty. He's already achieved so much as a manager and I'm sure he's going to go on to even bigger and better things. Strangely, though, I never saw him going into management. Scotty didn't like the politics that went with football and he's quite a reserved person. I recently asked him to do a video for a kid who loved him as a player and it took him 50 takes to record it because he was sweating so much. We laughed about it afterwards because it seemed like such a minor request, but that type of thing just didn't come naturally to him.

But we always knew that Scott would give his all on the pitch. We had a decent team and Jack Collison also gave us an extra layer of quality. Jack had so much talent. He was another academy product and his performances in training impressed Gianfranco, who appreciated the value of energising the senior squad by adding youth to the mix. James Tomkins, Zavon Hines, Freddie Sears and Junior Stanislas all had opportunities, and Jack did not take long to establish himself. Jack belonged at the highest level. He scored a great goal when we beat Manchester City 1–0 at the start of March and I'm convinced that he'd have played for a top-four club if his career hadn't been ruined by injury.

Jack didn't deserve such rotten luck. It was horrible seeing him go down in agony with a dislocated kneecap when we beat Wigan three days after our win over City. Jack ended up rushing back too soon, which shouldn't have been allowed to happen, and he was never the same again. It wasn't fair.

* * *

Football can be a brutal sport. We were outstanding against Wigan, winning in freezing conditions after Carlton Cole finished off a wonderful one-touch passing move, but my attention was elsewhere. Carly was heavily pregnant, and I realised that my life was about to change when I got back to the dressing room and saw a load of missed calls, which could only mean one thing: I was about to become a father.

I was all over the place. Carly had gone to hospital after feeling pain, her labour had started three weeks early and I was miles away from home. It wasn't looking good. We still had to drive back to Manchester airport for our flight back to London, which was delayed for an hour because they had to de-ice the plane before we could take off.

There was no way I was going to make it back in time. We landed at Stansted airport, got on the coach and answered a call from Carly's sister. I was too late. Carly needed an emergency C-section and I had to listen to the birth on the phone, my heart pounding when I heard our little baby girl let out her first cry.

I felt sick. I finally got to the hospital at 3 a.m. and held Honey in my arms. 'Nothing else matters,' I thought as I gazed at my first child. 'All the worries about football … it doesn't matter.'

I was in a daze. I woke up after a brief sleep and called Gianfranco, who told me to take a couple of hours off. I wandered around London on my own, buying anything that was pink, and tried to make sense of my emotions. I was only 21. A kid. What did I know about looking after a child? 'I've got a family now,' I thought. 'I've got to support them.'

Yet I couldn't be around with them as much as I'd have liked. Footballers don't take paternity leave. I had to maintain my fitness, and Gianfranco didn't let me stay at home when we went to Spain for a short training camp. It was difficult. The other players came with their families but it was too soon for Carly to bring Honey. I missed them terribly.

Football forces you to make sacrifices. Carly knew it was part of the job and she had help with the baby from her family, but it wasn't ideal. It hit me when I came back from Spain. I still had to train every day and it was like someone had chucked a grenade into the house. Carly had her hands full with Honey while I was trying to make sure that I was ready for Premier League football. It forced me to be selfish. Sleep was vital, so I couldn't do any night feeds. I look back now and regret behaving like a pig. I felt like I had to make sure that I provided for my family, but I didn't think more about Carly's needs. She was on her own in a big house and we had Lenny, our son, a year after Honey. Now we joke that we probably didn't have a real conversation for a few years. I would come home knackered from training every day, hoping to relax, only for Carly to ask me to take the kids off her hands while she had a bath.

Was it the healthiest way to live? Probably not – but what was I meant to do? I was behaving like any other footballer, and Gianfranco needed me to be available. After all, he didn't have many players at his disposal. We were playing well and were pleased to finish the season in ninth place, but the club was a mess. Players know when things aren't right. It feeds down from the top and we could tell that Gianfranco was struggling to deal with the owners.

The tone was set when our shirt sponsor, XL Airways, went bust at the start of the season. The solution was to iron a patch of claret over the logo on the front of our kit. We couldn't believe it. We were laughing our heads off but I wasn't happy. The next fix was to put our squad numbers on the front of our shirts. It was embarrassing. We looked like an amateur side and it hurt to see what was happening to my club.

The finances were in a shambolic state. The January transfer window brought more pain. Two experienced players, Matthew Etherington and Hayden Mullins, were sold, and there was no chance of us holding out when Manchester City came in for Bellers.

I couldn't blame Bellers for wanting to go to City. He was a huge loss and I wasn't impressed with how we replaced him. We didn't go for someone proven. Instead we bought a complete unknown, paying £9m to bring Savio Nsereko in from Brescia. It was a bizarre signing. Our sporting director, Gianluca Nani, had also joined us from Brescia, but we could tell straight away that Savio wasn't cut out to be our No9. It wasn't fair on him. He was just a kid and he didn't deserve to be thrown in to that situation.

That signing wasn't right. Gianfranco tried to make the best of it and did a lot of individual work with Savio after training, but he was fighting a losing battle. Football's about body language and Savio's entire demeanour told us that he wasn't what we needed. He had no confidence and it wasn't a surprise that he failed to make an impact for us, before joining Fiorentina at the end of the season.

We were baffled. Who does that after selling Craig Bellamy for £14m? We had a talented squad and could have pushed on if we'd spent the money wisely. Instead we wasted it and the team suffered. That was West Ham back then. I was angry. I might have spoken up if I'd been more experienced but in reality it was out of our control. 'Why have we gone and done that?' I thought. 'Why can't we do things properly?'

I was worried about where we were heading. There was no philosophy. No structure. Di Michele was a decent player but there was no logic to our recruitment. We signed the former Spain striker Diego Tristán on a free transfer but he wasn't in the right condition to play in the Premier League. Did anyone at the top care? They were just picking players off a tree in the hope they could fill a hole for a while. It was nothing more than damage limitation. We were merely papering over the cracks and at some point it was going to fall apart. A storm was brewing on the horizon.

5

Relegation

The rain continued to pour before the start of the 2009–10 season. If losing Lucas Neill on a free transfer was unfortunate, then failing to replace him by signing a new right-back was downright careless. Lucas was our captain and he was a top defender. It wasn't fair on Gianfranco. The club was in an increasingly bad state and he was beginning to show signs of strain, even though we made a deceptively good start to the season, convincingly beating Wolves 2–0 at Molineux in our opening game.

The victory papered over the cracks, however. I had an excellent game, putting us ahead in the first half by curling a shot into the top corner from 20 yards and helping us seal the points by whipping in a corner for Matty Upson to score our second goal, but the squad wasn't in a good shape. Gianfranco barely had any money to spend. He was forced to gamble, with Gianluca Nani focused on signing players from Italy. Whether the new arrivals were suited to the rough and tumble of English football didn't seem to be a consideration. We were losing experienced Premier League players and replacing them with cheap punts from abroad, so nobody could act surprised when we began to slide into trouble.

There was only so long that we could get away with it. The problems seeped down from the top and I didn't blame the new boys for our poor form. I loved playing with Guillermo Franco, who came in on a free transfer from Villarreal. He was an experienced striker, a Mexico international, a friendly guy and a top professional. He wanted to do well for West Ham and he loved the physical side of the game. Guillermo wasn't scared of grappling with opposition defenders and I admired his intelligence. He never tried to do anything fancy; I could trust him to hold the ball up, lay it off and bring others into play if I knocked it up to him.

We weren't a complete lost cause. We had some talent and I really liked our maverick Italian playmaker Alessandro Diamanti. He was a fiery character, a wild personality and the first player I ever saw bring a hairdryer into the dressing room. He was also an entertainer. Alessandro had a wand of a left foot, scored some cracking goals and was desperate to win. I respected him, and I know that he still speaks fondly of his spell at West Ham.

Yet the overall mix wasn't right. It was hard for Alessandro to move to a new country and flourish in that environment. Foreign players can easily get lost when they join a struggling club. I looked at Luis Jiménez, who joined us on loan from Internazionale, and felt sorry for him. He was a technically gifted forward and he tried his best, but the football didn't suit his game and he went back to Italy long before the season was over. How could anyone have thought that he was right for us?

We kept making bad decisions. We weakened our defence further by selling James Collins to Aston Villa, which was a huge blow, replacing him by bringing in Manuel da Costa from Fiorentina. I was mystified. Ginge had done brilliantly for us after signing from Cardiff in 2005 and wasn't afraid of putting his head where it hurt. He knew the league, and it was irritating to see him and Lucas go at the same time.

It was inevitable, therefore, that our performances suffered. Da Costa had big boots to fill. He was young, had a lot to learn and wasn't short of aggression. He spent most of his spare time playing *Call of Duty* and was a big, strong boy who ate rare steak for lunch every day. He certainly had the physical attributes to play in the Premier League and he wasn't a bad footballer. The problem is that we threw him in at the deep end. He was an inexperienced player in a crucial position and we quickly began to leak too many goals.

The mood at the club grew negative. We stopped winning games and I could feel the weight of expectation on my shoulders growing heavier. I wasn't seen as a kid any more and for the first time in my career people were looking at me to get us out of trouble, even though I was still in my early 20s. We lacked senior players and I knew that youngsters like Jack Collison, James Tomkins and Junior Stanislas were looking up to me. It felt suffocating. I cared about the club so much and I was desperate to save us, but it got on top of me as I wasn't used to dealing with so much pressure. I bumped into West Ham fans everywhere I went, so I was constantly being asked why we were playing this badly. It was difficult to know what to say. I just had to offer up some platitudes, and in the end I stopped going out. Subjecting myself to those conversations all the time wasn't doing me any favours.

It was draining. Things were difficult at home. I was never happy when West Ham were struggling and Carly wasn't having a great time either. She had her hands full with Honey and was already pregnant with our son Lenny. She needed more from me but football was pulling me away from my family. I didn't have the tools to cope and it probably affected my performances.

Nonetheless my private life wasn't the club's concern. West Ham needed me to step up and I was letting them down. I was in a rut. I was sent off for two bookings when we lost to Birmingham in November and found myself wondering where I was going wrong. I didn't know where to turn. I was lost and required someone to guide me back on to the right path. I needed help.

*   *   *

It's horrible when your confidence fades away. Everything becomes a struggle if you're low on self-belief. Every simple pass becomes a hard pass, every simple tackle feels like a risk, and my desperation to impress made me even worse. I thought that the only way forward was to try even harder, to push myself even more, to take on even more responsibility, but I was too inexperienced to realise that my eagerness to improve the situation wasn't helping.

I was simply digging myself an even bigger hole. I went looking for the ball in stupid areas, which doesn't solve anything when you're having a nightmare, and I reached a low point when we spiralled deeper into danger after losing 2–1 away to Burnley at the start of February.

I was awful. Gianfranco played me as a No10 and I had a shocker. My game was about knowing when to play a pass and not getting caught in possession. I wasn't comfortable playing with my back to goal, and Dad, who watched the game from the away end at Turf Moor and had to listen to the West Ham fans tearing into me, didn't shy away from the truth when he called me in the evening. 'Boy, what the f**k's going on with you?' he said. 'You just don't look like the same player.'

'I don't f**king know, Dad,' I said. 'I don't need this right now.'

We argued a bit but I knew he was right. I was gutted. I'd become utterly devoid of self-belief and needed someone to give me a fresh perspective. I'd never had much of an ego. I knew that a couple of the players used a sports psychologist, Mike Griffiths, and I wasn't too proud to ask him to work with me.

I had always felt invincible; now I was ready to be vulnerable. 'A career in football is not a smooth journey,' I tell players now. 'It's a horrible mixture of emotions and you've got to be able to handle them. You've got to know how to address it when things aren't going well.'

I would recommend Mike to anyone. He made me a much better player and I continued working with him until I retired, even inviting him to my wedding. I valued his advice so much. He changed the way I viewed football and gave me a different outlook on life. We usually spoke the night before a game and would talk about how I'd been training. We looked at what I needed to work on, then I'd go back to him a day after the game to talk about what had gone well and where I needed to improve.

It was useful to listen to a different voice. I felt clearer after talking to Mike as he knew how to make me analyse my game. If I told him that I'd played well he'd say, 'Well, why did you play well? What did you do? How did you prepare? And what didn't you do? What didn't you do so well and what can you do to make sure you don't do that again?'

Carly could see that the sessions improved me. She took the piss sometimes, telling me to ring Mike whenever I got angry, but she knew that I'd become a happier person. Mike always stressed the importance of family, and I think that my sessions with him made life at home better.

I was now a lot calmer during matches. I came to realise that it was a mistake to take the ball in bad areas of the pitch – I wasn't helping the team and I was only going to get myself in trouble. I became less naive. I went through a tough time, and another type of player might have decided that they couldn't take it any more. They might have concluded that they needed an easier life and moved on to a different club, but I could never go down that route. I was fully committed to West Ham and I didn't have a bad game for the rest of that season. If you're not good enough you lose your place, and I kept mine because

I was consistent. I just needed to sort myself out and trust that my form would return.

*   *   *

I'm better at processing my emotions now. I've learnt that it helps to get things off your chest. If I can deal with something difficult then I tackle it. If it's out of my control then I've realised that there isn't much point stressing too much about it.

I try not to let things fester in my head. And I cry all the time. I get genuinely emotional when I see good things happen to people. I always became emotional when some- one started crying after advancing to the next round of *The X Factor*. I was on a plane home once, watching a docu- mentary about Justin Bieber, and got really teary when they brought a girl who was a Justin Bieber superfan on stage. 'What the f**k is going on with me?' I thought.

I don't know why it happens to me. I was far more stub- born when I was younger. I was reluctant to show my emotions, even though I was going through a challenging time. My form was rubbish and I was envious when I saw my mates going out in the evening. I was 22 and just wanted to have some fun, but I had a young family and needed to be professional. It was difficult to let off some steam. Carly and I were like a lot of young parents:

exhausted, stressed out and struggling to find enough time for each other.

We were incredibly grateful to our neighbours, Tina and Jeff Pope, for helping out. They have three boys and are older than us. Jeff's a really successful writer who's had some hit shows on TV, and they gave us so much support that we made them godparents to our kids.

Things became easier after a while. Yet while my form was better, our relegation fears were deepening. The squad was stretched by injuries, we couldn't put a run together and the club's financial situation was dreadful. The owners had run out of money and there were suggestions that the club would fall into administration unless there was a take-over.

It's impossible for a club to function properly under these kinds of constraints. Too many mistakes had been made, too many corners had been cut. As players, we knew that the situation was serious but it was out of our control. We weren't the ones in charge of the money. All we could do was try to remain professional by getting on with the job of winning games, which we weren't doing very well. But in reality the only way to avoid financial Armageddon was for our Icelandic owners to sell up before it was too late.

The anxiety remained even after David Sullivan and David Gold completed their takeover in January 2010.

They soon realised that they had a hell of a job on their hands. Relegation was on the cards, so they weren't afraid to ruffle a few feathers. They spoke out and such blunt talk didn't go down well at the time, although I later realised that the owners were already fretting about their investment.

They had inherited a mess and were worried about dropping down into the Championship. I can't blame them for panicking. The squad was unbalanced, we were playing terribly and the atmosphere at Upton Park was toxic when we got smashed by Wolves at the end of March. I started on the bench and couldn't believe what I was watching. 'F**king hell,' I thought as Wolves went 3–0 up. 'I'm glad I'm not out there.'

That defeat was the lowest point of Gianfranco's time at West Ham. We were just above the bottom three but we looked like we were never going to win again. David Sullivan and David Gold had arrived just before the end of the January transfer window and they didn't have to much time to strengthen the squad, the search for more firepower in attack ending with us bringing in Benni McCarthy, Ilan and Mido.

I'm a people person. I try to get on with everyone and Benni, Ilan and Mido were all nice guys. But if I'm in recruitment I'm making a point of seeing if a player actually cares about making West Ham successful. You can't just sign someone in the vague hope that they hit the ground running and score a few goals. The source of their motivation matters, and there have been too many occasions over the years when we've fallen into the trap of signing players who knew their best days were behind them and were drawn to us because they wanted to have a bit of fun in London.

We were signing memories when it came to Benni and Mido. Benni was a top striker in his day and he certainly wasn't short of self-belief on the pitch, as I discovered when I sent him flying with a firm challenge during a game against Blackburn in 2007. 'How dare you tackle me?' he said after landing on top of me, which I thought was hilarious.

This was a player who'd won the Champions League with Porto in 2004. Benni had undoubted quality and I can see why we decided to gamble on him and Mido, but it soon became clear that they weren't the right signings for us. They weren't quick enough for the Premier League any more and neither of them scored for West Ham. However, I don't blame Mido for joining us. He didn't sign himself and I got on with him, although it was a mistake to stand aside and let him take a penalty when we drew with Everton at the start of April. The fans were fuming when Mido's effort was easily saved by Tim Howard. It was another example of our indiscipline as a squad. We didn't have a clear-cut order for set-pieces and that was asking for trouble, given that the dressing room was full of players who wanted to take all the penalties, all the free-kicks and probably all the throw-ins.

There were some big egos in the squad and they probably saw me as a kid who could be easily shoved aside. Diamanti took a couple of penalties instead of me when I was on the pitch, and it was only when Sam Allardyce took over and signed Kevin Nolan to be his captain that the debates ended over my role as our penalty taker. I appreciated having clarity because I didn't want to argue with my team-mates during a game. I found public disagreements embarrassing. I just bit my tongue and let them get on with it. Looking back, it isn't hard to see why we were fighting for survival all the time.

*　　*　　*

Relegation battles are horrible. There's no escape from the fear of failure, no respite from the tension. It consumes every part of your life. You worry about letting the fans down and fret about staff at the club losing their livelihoods. You end up watching other struggling sides play on TV, praying that they'll help you out by losing. You spend hours gazing at the table, fruitlessly working out how many points it will take to stay up, and you try to give yourself hope by looking at the fixtures and telling yourself, 'If we beat them and they lose to them we might be all right …'

It isn't a fun existence. The thought of going down affected me acutely. I don't know if it was the same for other players but it hit me hard. I was a homegrown player, everyone in my life supported West Ham, and I felt like people were looking at me and thinking, 'Come on, then, f**king do something – what are you going to do to get us out of this shit?'

My emotions were a mixture of anger and frustration. I thought that West Ham were a big enough club not to have to go through so much turmoil year after year. Our inability to live up to our potential hurt me. Equally, though, it was delusional to think that we were a good team. We went through some desperate times during that season. Players kept getting injured – nothing summed our luck up more than Guillermo Franco getting an infection in his Achilles after he stepped on a thorn during a round of golf – and at one point me and Scotty were feeling so pessimistic about our chances of staying up that we found ourselves trying to convince Gianfranco to give us a boost by coming out of retirement.

That's how bad it was: two senior players asking their 44-year-old manager to put himself up front. I joked about it with Scotty on the coach home after another demoralising defeat but the idea wasn't as ridiculous as it sounds. Gianfranco had kept himself fit and he was still so classy when he trained with us. What did we have to lose? We didn't have enough players and we thought that it was worth a try. 'Boss, why don't you just register yourself as a player,' I said. 'You're still one of the best players in training. You might have to make yourself available. Even if you come on for the last 20 minutes, you could make a difference.'

Gianfranco thought that we were having a laugh. He tried to bat it away but we weren't joking any more. 'We're serious,' I said. 'We're just telling you the truth. You're still good enough to change a game if you come off the bench.'

But the idea never got off the ground. Gianfranco just laughed at us and found it all a bit embarrassing. 'No, don't be silly,' he said. 'I'm retired. I'm not coming back. I'm the manager now.'

There was no way Gianfranco was going to change his mind. We had to forget about it and do the job ourselves. We still had hope and we managed to grind out a couple of crucial wins during the run-in. Ilan chipped in with a few vital goals, including the winner when we beat Sunderland 1–0, and we were finally safe after earning a nervy 3–2 win over Wigan at the end of April, Scotty coming to the rescue when he combined with Guillermo and banged in a brilliant shot from 25 yards.

It was pure relief when Scotty scored that goal. We'd dug in and done enough to cling on to our place in the top flight. When it came to the crunch we still had sufficient talent and there was just about enough experience in the squad to ensure that the dressing room didn't become totally toxic. Our effort certainly was never the issue. We trained well, and because we liked and respected Gianfranco we wanted to play for him.

Yet it was clear that the season had taken a heavy toll on Gianfranco. He had to cope with losing key players because of our awful financial situation and there was constant speculation about his future. It came as no surprise when the two Davids sacked him at the end of the season. He wasn't their appointment and they wanted to bring in their own man.

It was a shame that it had to end that way for Gianfranco, although – and I mean this as a compliment – he was probably too nice a person to be a manager. He's a lovely man, a gentle soul, and he wanted to help everyone reach their potential. It was a pleasure to play for him. Gianfranco had time for everyone and I spent a lot of time working with him individually, practising free-kicks and going through shooting drills after training. His advice mattered to me and I was extremely sad to see him go. Gianfranco was more than a manager; he was – and remains – a friend. I'm still in touch with him now and nobody could question his desire to make West Ham successful. He tried his best in extremely taxing circumstances and never, ever showed any sign of losing his dignity.

I don't even think that he did a bad job. We finished ninth in his first season and his best was enough to keep us up in his second year. Yet management is a harsh business. Ultimately managers can't be friends with their players. They have to be ready to drop players and dig them out, but that wasn't Gianfranco's style. His skill was building connections with people. He cared about players to the point where it became his undoing. Gianfranco didn't want to hammer his players, but sometimes there's no other choice. It's a tough job and players need to be made aware when they're not playing well.

Yet ruthlessness didn't come naturally to Gianfranco. In the end his innocence and romanticism cost him. He was still learning his trade and would have benefited from starting his career at a less chaotic club. Upton Park was no place for a rookie manager. The amount of pressure on Gianfranco wasn't fair and the owners probably did him a favour when they fired him.

There was no doubt that we needed a fresh approach after finishing 17th and picking up a paltry 35 points. Deep down I knew that we were lucky to stay up. 'F**king hell, we've got away with that this year,' I thought. 'We were shit.' There wasn't much to celebrate. We were fortunate that the three teams who did go down – Burnley, Hull and Portsmouth – were so weak. I was under no illusions when I went away on holiday. 'We need to pick the right manager and sign some decent players,' I thought. 'We can't go on like this. It's asking to go wrong eventually.' I knew that a difficult road lay stretched out ahead. The question was whether we were ready for another fight.

*   *   *

I desperately wanted to believe that the dark times were over for West Ham. I wanted the club's pain to end and I allowed myself to feel excited before the start of the 2010–11 season. The owners were beginning to settle in and their decision to replace Gianfranco with Avram Grant, who had a good reputation after almost winning the Champions League with Chelsea in 2008, seemed like a wise move after we won all of our friendlies during pre-season. 'Come on, this might actually be good,' I thought. 'New owners, new manager … maybe we really are about to turn the corner.'

Sadly, my optimism was misplaced as the task ahead was steep. There was a bit of hype, a bit of hope, and all it took to shatter the positive vibes was for us to play one competitive game. It was like someone had slapped me in the face, making me snap out of it and realise that I was living in a fantasy world, and it wasn't too soon to panic when we lost 3–0 to Aston Villa on the opening day. We were miles off the pace, utterly disorganised without the ball, and I could already tell that it was going to be another long, gruelling, dispiriting season

'We are way off it,' I thought. 'We are absolutely nowhere near where we need to be if we want to stay in this league. Nothing's changed – we're just as bad as we were last season.'

It felt horrendous. We needed to hit the reset button. Things still weren't right. The squad was a strange mix of flavours, none of which went together, and the writing was on the wall after we followed up the defeat to Villa by losing our next three games.

We were already back in survival mode. Avram wanted us to play expansive football, but we were nowhere near as talented as the players he'd had at Chelsea. What we needed was a manager who could make us hard to beat. A manager who knew how to hold on to a lead and nick a game 1–0. A manager like Sam Allardyce, who would have focused on the basics, taught us how to scrap and made sure that getting points on the board was more important than trying to keep the crowd entertained.

But that wasn't Avram's philosophy. He was available after a nightmare year at Portsmouth, whose financial difficulties had led to them dropping down into the Championship, and I don't think he was up for another relegation battle. Avram didn't have a set way of playing. He wrote some core fundamentals up on a board but they didn't leave a lasting impression. The entire approach was vague, and we ended up straying away from West Ham's tradition of working hard and playing as one.

We weren't good enough to play off the cuff. The focus should have been on getting results. We needed to be told what to do and when to do it, but Avram didn't involve himself much in coaching. He let his backroom staff take charge of training and mostly kept out of sight.

Yet despite his difficulties at West Ham I didn't resent Avram. Our problems weren't solely down to him. The rot had set in long before he arrived and I didn't envy him walking into such a terrible situation. West Ham is an unforgiving place when you're losing all the time, and the fans weren't happy with any of us. We tried to rouse ourselves, but I feared the worst when we ended up rooted to the bottom of the table after getting smashed by Chelsea at the start of September. It was a fatal combination of shattered confidence, a lack of anything approaching a team structure, and players looking at each other and thinking, 'We're f**ked.'

We didn't have a bad dressing room, it was just that the lads were sick to death of fighting relegation. We were on a slippery slope and the mood around the club was one of utter deflation. There were a few flashes, a few hints of us putting a run together, and we were capable of playing some decent football on the rare occasions when everything went our way. We fully deserved the three points when we earned our first win of the season by beating Tottenham at Upton Park at the end of September. Victor Obinna and Freddie Piquionne were a handful up front. We created loads of chances and for once we defended well, holding on to our lead after I swung in a corner for Freddie to score the only goal of the game.

I was on top of the world after full-time. I was so elated I ended up asking Carly to marry me when we went out for dinner in the evening. I'd had the ring for a few weeks and decided there was no better time to propose than after a win over Spurs, which wasn't exactly the most romantic of gestures. Honey came to the restaurant with us and, to my eternal shame, I didn't even get down on one knee. I just blurted out the question from across the table and have spent our entire marriage making it up to Carly, even though I wasn't worried about the possibility of her turning me down. Carly cried when she saw the ring, and because we'd been together so long I knew she was going to say yes.

I didn't have to hold my breath. We already had a family and I saw beating Spurs as a bigger achievement than getting engaged. It was a rare highlight in a wretched season, though it turned out to be a false dawn. It was typical of our luck when Kieron Dyer limped off before half-time against Spurs after causing them loads of problems on the right wing. Kieron had never fully recovered from breaking his leg on his debut for us in 2007 and he simply couldn't take the strain of playing in the Premier League any more. His talent was intact but his body wasn't cooperating. I was gutted for him. We could have done with a fit-and-firing Kieron Dyer. We needed all the help we could get at that stage.

*   *   *

There was no consistency to our play. We were far too open, gave away too many leads and were pushed around too easily by physical sides. It wasn't hard to score against us. Newcastle didn't have to do anything special when they won 2–1 at Upton Park. We went 1–0 up early on but we had no way of handling Andy Carroll and Kevin Nolan. Andy terrorised us with his ability in the air and strength on the ground. At one stage I did him with a Cruyff turn and it sounded like I was being chased by a buffalo. The noises coming out of Andy's mouth made as he stomped after me in his size 12 Umbro boots were absurd. I was convinced he was going to smash me. I was absolutely shitting myself, and I wasn't surprised when he scored the winner, meeting a wicked cross from Joey Barton with an unstoppable header.

We had none of that oomph. We trundled along, flattering to deceive, throwing away a series of winnable home games. It was one of the few times in my career that I found no enjoyment in football. The season was a slog, even though my form was fine. We went to Arsenal at the end of October, frustrated them with a battling performance and still lost in the last minute. A few days later I woke up with a searing pain in my stomach. My first thought was that Carly's cooking had given me food poisoning.

'Those prawns made me ill,' I said before leaving the house, but I realised that something far more serious was happening when I collapsed at training.

'You've got to go to hospital now,' the club doctor said after poking two fingers into my stomach and making me scream in agony. 'Your appendix is about to burst.'

I had to have surgery that day and I was out of action for a few weeks. It made me feel useless. The lads were losing all the time and I was unable to affect anything. I watched us beat Manchester United 4–0 in the quarter-finals of the League Cup, with Jonathan Spector scoring twice and playing like Messi in midfield, but I also saw a lot of underwhelming performances. We kept missing opportunities to put points on the board and the newspapers were full of rumours about the board planning to sack Avram, who looked like he wanted to be put out his misery by the time January arrived.

I'm not sure how Avram managed to cling on to his job. The owners were known for sticking by their managers, and although our survival appeared to hinge on them hiring a new manager, they stuck with Avram. We showed some defiance when we hosted Birmingham in the first leg of our League Cup semi-final at the start of January, grinding out a 2–1 win despite losing Obinna to a red card during the second half, but the speculation only became more intense as we tried to think about facing Arsenal at Upton Park the following Saturday. Was Avram staying or going? Were the rumours about Martin O'Neill coming in true? While nobody expected us to beat Arsenal, it hardly put us in the right frame of mind when we woke up on Saturday morning to reports claiming that the board had decided to sack Avram and replace him with O'Neill even if we won the game.

The mood around the ground was flat and we played like a team of schoolboys, offering up little resistance as Arsenal demolished us 3–0. Then, to make matters worse, O'Neill turned us down. We were back to square one. Avram was going nowhere, even though the board clearly didn't back him, and we had no option but to plough on with him in the dugout.

Nothing went right. We went up to Birmingham for the second leg of our League Cup semi-final and looked set to make it to Wembley after Carlton Cole put us 3–1 up on aggregate in the first half, only to collapse in the second half and lose the tie in extra-time. We tried to use the transfer window to our advantage but the squad was a mess. It was going to take more than a few panic buys to sort us out this time.

There were faint glimmers of hope. Thomas Hitzlsperger made us better in midfield after returning from a long-term injury, while we improved our attack by signing Demba Ba from Hoffenheim and taking Robbie Keane from Spurs on loan. I really enjoyed playing with Robbie. His movement was unreal, his touch was superb and he gave us a massive boost by scoring on his debut when we beat Blackpool at the start of February. Then he missed the next two months after tearing his calf during yet another defeat to Birmingham.

We were constantly taking one step forward and two steps back. We went to West Brom at the end of February and stank the place out during the first half. We were 3–0 down at half-time and Scotty was so angry he ended up taking the team-talk during the break. 'Lads, listen, if you don't want to play, just don't play,' he said. 'There's no point. You need to actually go out there and f**king get a bit of pride back because that was f**king embarrassing.'

Scotty's words struck a chord. We were a different team in the second half and fought back to earn a point thanks to goals from Demba and Coley. Suddenly we had some momentum. We beat Liverpool 3–1 at home and picked up a solid point against Spurs. Yet it never felt like we were going to pull off another great escape. The writing was on the wall after we chucked away a 2–0 lead against United at the start of April. I scored two penalties during the first half but the only thing going through my mind during half-time was, 'F**k, we've still got to hold out against this lot for another 45 minutes.'

I never fancied us to protect a lead. We couldn't do it against Birmingham in the cup and we had no clue how to respond when United quickened the pace during the second half. It was a horrible feeling. Fear took over. We dropped deeper and deeper, gave the ball away too much and watched in awe as Wayne Rooney turned the game around by scoring a phenomenal hat-trick.

'I'm not sure we're ever going to win a game again,' I thought. We didn't deserve anything. We lost our next two games badly, and then my season was over after I did my hernia during a 3–0 defeat to Chelsea at the end of April. I cut inside, took a shot and immediately felt it snap. I was in so much pain, and needed Didier Drogba to help me off the pitch.

Surgery was the only option. I couldn't travel with the team when we visited Wigan in our penultimate game, knowing that only a win would keep us in with a chance of staying up on the final day. It was a dismal afternoon. Avram was sacked straight after the game, the board having been left with no other choice after our relegation was sealed by a shambolic 3–2 defeat, and the boys said it was pretty strange to see him on the team bus on the way home. It was one more indignity in a season full of them.

I just wanted it to be over by that stage. We made a powderpuff show of getting a result against Wigan, two goals from Demba giving us a 2–0 lead at the break, but it was the same old story after half-time. The fight had disappeared and we all knew what to expect in the second half.

'Just get it over and done with,' I thought. I simply wanted the humiliations to stop. I felt sorry for the people around the training ground, the people whose jobs were most at risk because of our rubbish performances, but my overriding emotion was relief. I saw going down as a blessing in disguise. We couldn't blame bad luck or dodgy refereeing decisions. The fact is that it was always going to end this way. This relegation was three years in the making and I wasn't interested in excuses. None of us were good enough and there was only one way to react now we were a Championship club: rip it all up, start again and get ready to repair the damage.

6

Big Sam's
Tough Love

There was a part of me that thought, 'We f**king deserve it' when I watched us get relegated. We embarrassed ourselves by finishing bottom of the league, and I expected the worst when we held an end-of-season awards ceremony at the Grosvenor House Hotel in central London.

The mood was tense. We were fed up and the fans were irritated by our lack of enthusiasm. 'Oi,' one of them said, 'what's the matter with you lot?'

It was exactly what I was worried about. The fans had been drinking and tempers were already strained. We needed to choose our words carefully, but Demba Ba hadn't read the warning signs.

'It's late,' Demba said. 'I'm tired.'

'F**king tired! We've been watching this shit for nine f**king months and you're tired!'

The conversation was over. 'We probably deserved it,' I thought. 'We played like shit.'

I could have walked away at that stage. I got away from the negativity by going on holiday with Carly and the kids, but I knew that my time at West Ham could be up. Our best players were obviously up for sale and my agent was on at me all the time, asking what I wanted to do next. Fulham were linked with me and I was a bit confused. My contract was running out, I was emotionally drained after three really tough years, and people around me were telling me to go. 'You need to leave,' they said. 'You need to go and play in the Premier League. What happens if you don't go up? You've got to think about what's best for your career.'

These were valid arguments, and there was a lot of speculation about my future when I came back from holiday. I didn't want to play in the Championship. I'd given my heart and soul to West Ham, but was it time to be ruthless? Was it time to put myself first and seek a new challenge?

It wouldn't have been hard to find a new club. Ultimately, though, I never had talks with anyone about leaving. I thought back to the comfort and security West Ham had provided when I was going through difficult times in my private life. I thought about local pride and how much the community meant to me. This was home; my second family.

I needed to give it another go. I owed it to West Ham to stay. We still had a decent squad and I was encouraged when we appointed Sam Allardyce as our new manager at the start of June, although initially I wasn't sure if I was his kind of player. He signed Kevin Nolan, who was great for Sam at Bolton, and I wondered if there was going to be space for me in midfield.

But those doubts didn't last long. I wasn't invited to give my view when Sam hauled me into his office. 'Listen, you ain't going anywhere,' he said. 'Forget it. We need to get promoted and I need you here. Give us another year. I think we can do it.'

I didn't need any more convincing. I was buzzing. I thought we had a chance of making things right, and once I stopped thinking about leaving I became obsessed with getting us back where we belonged.

Sam was building a strong, physical side, even though he lost Demba, Thomas Hitzlsperger and Scotty Parker. Kev took the captain's armband following the departure of Matthew Upson, and we had a solid core of experienced professionals. Sam knew he could rely on me, Kev, Robert Green, Matty Taylor and Joey O'Brien to ensure that standards remained high in the dressing room.

It was about changing the club's identity and becoming more resilient. I had to adjust my thinking after we lost our opening game at home to Cardiff. It was no longer about fancy football or putting on a show for the crowd – the Championship wasn't as technical as the Premier League. We bounced back a week later, grinding out a 1–0 win away to Doncaster Rovers. We didn't play well, but Kev and Big Sam were buzzing because they knew getting a result mattered more than anything else.

Sam had a reputation for playing direct football. His Bolton side sent West Ham down in 2003, and people wondered if the fans at Upton Park would take to his style of play. But I didn't care. We needed a manager like him to get us out of the Championship. We needed someone who wouldn't take any nonsense, a manager who could give us stability and turn us into a team that knew how to win ugly.

We were like a tortoise with no shell before Sam arrived. If I had one word to describe us it would be 'soft'. We got done over every week. Our confidence was shot to pieces after three years of losing leads under Gianfranco and Avram. We hadn't spent enough time working on the defensive side of the game and the club was in turmoil because of the damage done by previous owners. We needed Sam to put us back together.

* * *

Sam made us tough. He grabbed hold of Winston Reid, who struggled badly under Avram, and worked tirelessly on turning him into a top centre-back. Sam could see his potential and he didn't want to write him off. Winston was an excellent athlete, powerful in the air and so much better now he was being guided by Sam, whose coaching also had a really positive impact on James Tomkins's performances in central defence.

We finally began to tighten up and stop conceding silly goals. Winston and Tonks had a great partnership at the back, and we were making our physical power count at the other end. There was far more work on set-pieces. We had plenty of big lads – Tonks was always a threat at the back post, giving me a safety net if I ever overhit a dead ball – and Sam made sure I had clear instructions about where to send our corners and free-kicks.

Sam was obsessed with stats. He had all the numbers worked out and was constantly saying we'd get goals if we kept putting the ball in the right areas. Sam's clarity restored our confidence and I didn't mind altering my game for him. Under Avram it was all about playing the ball short, but Sam cared about efficiency. Kev was always waiting for the ball to run free in the box, and because Sam knew I had a good range of passing he was constantly on at me about knocking the ball in behind for our forward players to run on to and make chances.

It did my head in at times. It was relentless at training – 'Put it in behind, Nobes … you're not doing it enough' – Sam never stopped going on about it. He pissed me off so much. I was good at playing the ball into space, and towards the end of the season, when we were having breakfast in the team hotel before setting off for a big away game, I read an article that said no midfielder in the Championship had played more successful passes behind the opposition's defence than me.

'This'll show him,' I thought as I ripped the page out. I had to make my point. I got on the team coach to the game, slammed the article down in front of Sam and walked down to the other end without saying a word.

'You f**king cheeky c**t,' he bellowed.

Looking back, I'm not sure if I did actually get the better of him. It was great reverse psychology from Sam, whose man-management was second to none. He knew he had a trustworthy dressing room, and because we were winning most weeks we could get away with having an incredible social life. We went out loads as a team, and if we ever took the piss you could guarantee it that Sam would sit down next to us at breakfast and say, 'You must think I'm f**king stupid, youse lot.'

Sam always knew when we were up to no good. The training ground was a small place and staff always reported back to him. We never lied to him but we didn't listen when he told us not to go out during the week. It followed a particular routine: he'd say no, we'd do it anyway, he'd bollock us the next morning. 'Youse lot f**king better win on Saturday,' he'd say, 'otherwise you're all f**king fined.'

Of course, he never actually fined us. It was just a threat, and I don't think Sam cared that much. In fact I think he understood that going out and having a few beers improved our team spirit. A lot of my memories from football are not from the pitch but from the bonding trips and the nights out. You don't really know a team-mate until you leave the training ground, have a drink and open up a bit. Footballers are stuck in a bubble. You work so hard on staying fit and making sure you're ready to win the next game, so sometimes it's a good release to go out and have a laugh.

Carly expected it when I was younger. 'You going out with the boys tonight?' she'd ask if we got a big win on a Saturday afternoon. She knew we'd worked hard all week to get a result and, as long as we didn't have a midweek game, we deserved to celebrate. We deserved an opportunity to act like normal people.

That said, I never abused my body. I've never put a cigarette in my mouth and I made a decision early on in my career that I was going to dedicate myself to football. The only time when I went close to taking it too far was when I was beginning to establish myself in the first team. I was earning decent money for the first time, people were beginning to notice me and I acted like a bit of a prick. I liked being recognised and I didn't think twice about leaving Carly on her own at home.

Some players never snap out of that lifestyle. I always had a subconscious feeling that it wasn't for me. It wasn't right for my career or my relationship, so I pulled back. You always want what you can't have in life, but I wasn't jealous of my mates from home when they went out. I could have followed them, but then I wouldn't have lived out my dream. I'd have sabotaged myself.

Players are more professional these days, but they still drink from time to time. Even the foreign lads love it. It will catch up with you if you do it too much, but once or twice a month isn't a problem. You're under so much pressure to perform and win. It's incredibly stressful to live like that, so going out for a few beers and forgetting about football for a few hours is beautiful.

This wasn't lost on Sam. He knew how to manage players and get the best out of people. He treated us as individuals. He knew how to deal with Carlton Cole's horrendous timekeeping. Coley would bowl in late to training and say, 'Boss, sorry … I was out last night,' and Sam would just slag him off without turning it into a major crisis. Sam was smart: he knew he needed Coley on the weekend. Why make a fuss over something so minor?

* * *

It was give and take with Sam. His approach was simple: 'You give me points and I'll give you freedom. Otherwise I'm going to f**king take it away from you.'

We found that out the hard way when we went to Arsenal on a Wednesday evening during our first season back in the Premier League and got smashed 5–1. We waited an age for Sam to get on the coach after the game and he quickly silenced us when he finally turned up. 'You f**kers think you're funny,' he said. 'You made me watch that shit. So you're going to watch that shit at six in the morning.'

Sam wasn't joking. We were back at the training ground at the crack of dawn, all of us bleary eyed, and he was waiting for us. 'You think you're clever,' he said as he put the game on. 'Well, you can watch this now.'

It was miserable. Sam hammered us for ages, saying we were shit, his flow interrupted only when Coley turned up an hour late. 'Sorry, boss,' he said. 'I went out.' We all laughed. Sam just shook his head and carried on, torturing us until Kev stood up after about 80 minutes and said, 'Come on, gaffer, we've seen enough now.'

We were absolutely starving. It was 7.30 a.m. and Sam finally took pity on us. 'Go on,' he said. 'F**k off.' Then he joined us at breakfast, acting like nothing had happened.

It was in the past and Sam was already having a laugh about something else.

We could have a back and forth with Sam. He used to have fearsome rows about tactics with me and Kev in the dressing room. Kev stuck up for his team-mates all the time, and Sam was great at picking a fight out of nothing. We went to Man City in 2015 and couldn't get out of our own area. We were 2–0 down at half-time and Sam tore into us back in the dressing room, screaming at us to put the ball in behind and shouting at Coley for not stretching their defence enough.

'Hang on,' I said. 'How can he run in behind when we're playing on our 18-yard box? Why don't you f**king try running in behind against this lot?'

'You flash little c**t,' Sam said. 'I f**king would if I could.'

That was Sam all over. He loved a bit of banter in the dressing room, and he made sure it was full of reliable characters when we were trying to win promotion during our first season. He trusted Kev to be his captain and knew he could play his football.

The aim wasn't to be intricate when we were in the Championship. Kev wasn't fussed about taking the ball off the back four and dictating the play. I used to watch him on *Match of the Day* and think, 'You lucky bastard, how do you keep scoring so many goals?', but when he came to

West Ham I realised it was because he was always in the right place at the right time.

I had a good connection with Kev. I used him as a wall during games. I'd pop the ball around the corner to him, he'd set it off for me, and then he'd get himself into goal-scoring positions. The balance worked because I was ready to sit deeper. 'Kev, just get in the box,' I said. 'I'll do everything else. You just think about scoring.'

Kev was such a good player. Some people underestimate him but you don't play 400 games in the Premier League if you have no talent. He was strong, fit and he trained well every day. He didn't mind doing the dirty work, he always got forward, his finishing was unreal for a midfielder and his movement in the box was so smart.

He was annoying, too. He loved backing into opposition goalkeepers at corners, preventing them from coming out to catch the ball, and he was great at winding me up during small-sided games at training. We were never allowed to be on the same side because we both moaned at the referee so much, and Kev knew that the best way to stop my team playing was by man-marking me. 'Kev, I used to hate you,' I told him recently. 'As soon as training finished I used to think, "Please don't f**king come and stand on me."'

It was so frustrating. Kev's a big guy and because we were playing on a small pitch he made it impossible for me to get on the ball. I moaned about it to Neil McDonald, Sam's assistant, but he just told me to get on with it. It wasn't against the rules. He'd just stick to me and as soon as his team won possession he'd run off and score. Then he'd be back at my side when the game resumed.

'Kev, f**k off,' I said. 'Just let me enjoy the game.'

'Nah,' he replied. 'If I do that I know you're going to create everything for your team.'

It was a mistake to let Kev know he was getting on my nerves as it made him more determined to keep on doing it. He wasn't trying to help me become better tactically. He did it because it pissed me off and he wanted to win.

At least it was easier when players man-marked me in the Championship. The pitch was bigger, so I had more space, though I still found the smothering tactics infuriating.

'Mate, you're a footballer,' I said to one opponent. 'Go and enjoy the game.'

'I can't,' he replied. 'I've got to mark you. It's my job.'

*　　*　　*

A season in the Championship is a long old slog. We quickly established ourselves as a force on the road, our power at set-pieces earning us crushing victories away to Nottingham Forest and Watford during August, but we were more inconsistent at home. It wasn't easy to break down teams who came to Upton Park with the sole intention of frustrating us. We had a lot more of the ball, which was enjoyable for a player like me, but we were always under pressure to keep our fans happy by scoring the first goal. 'God, this must be what it feels like for teams like Man City and Man United,' I thought. 'Nobody wants to attack against us. They just want to see if they can hold out and make life difficult for us.'

It was a new challenge. In the Premier League we'd go away to the big clubs, sit back and try to nick a goal on the counterattack. Now the boot was on the other foot. The onus was on us to attack, and because we were West Ham the fans expected us to turn up and win every week.

Yet the Championship was never going to be that straightforward. There are a lot of proud clubs in that division and they all wanted to give us a bloody nose. Teams raised their game against us and we dropped some silly points at home, much to the frustration of our supporters.

Obviously Sam didn't panic. He believed in us and kept stressing that an average of two points per game would be enough to earn automatic promotion. All that mattered was finishing in the top two. Sam was pragmatic – he wasn't going to pay any attention if fans grumbled about our style of play.

But the problem for Sam was that we couldn't quite make the quality in our squad count. It took him a while to work out his best side. A lot of players had left after we were relegated and Sam had been forced to chuck a team together faster than he'd have liked. Time wasn't on his side and he hadn't been brought in for a gradual rebuild.

Our recruitment was therefore geared towards buying players who could come in and make an instant impact. It meant that Sam had to take a few punts. He made additions up front by signing Sam Baldock, who did quite well for us, and bringing in big John Carew, who scored a couple of important goals. But signing David Bentley on loan from Spurs didn't work out. Bents was a top lad and we had a great time at the Christmas party, but he was already falling out of love with football. His heart wasn't in it and his time with us ended prematurely when he suffered a bad knee injury in training.

We could have done with a player as creative as Bents in some of those tricky home games. Yet on the whole we were moving in the right direction. We were always in the top two and it looked like Southampton were the only side who could stop us winning the league.

Sam was changing our mentality. We didn't roll over when the going got tough, and the best example of our steel came when we hosted Millwall at the start of February. Nobody expected anything from us when Kev got himself sent off for a silly challenge after nine minutes. But that worked in our favour. The pressure was off and we put in a superb effort, digging deep to win 2–1 thanks to a volley from Winston in the second half.

We wouldn't have pulled off that result under Sam's predecessors. Going down to 10 men didn't scare us. It happened again in our next game, Matty Taylor picking up an early red card against Southampton after he clashed with Billy Sharp, and we held on for a 1–1 draw. We backed ourselves to cope without the ball. We were experienced and we knew our shape. We even survived when we had to put a midfielder in goal after losing Robert Green to a red card against Blackpool at the end of February. For some reason we didn't have a keeper on the bench, so Henri Lansbury calmly picked up the gloves and we went on to win the game 4–1.

Those backs-to-the-wall efforts gave us even more self-belief ahead of the run-in. It seemed promotion was nailed on. It didn't look like anyone other than Southampton could keep up with us.

But we weren't ready for Reading's surge. They emerged from nowhere to put an incredible winning run together and we let them in by drawing five games on the bounce in March. Suddenly fingers were being pointed at Sam. He was constantly being asked for his thoughts about the 'West Ham way', and his relationship with the fans was fragile. They didn't think that Sam respected the club's reputation for playing attacking football and he wasn't interested in taking their criticism.

Sam had skin as thick as a rhino. He didn't care what people said about his teams and he enjoyed causing controversy. He called the fans deluded and said they all talked bollocks. Sam loved winding people up and whipping up a storm. He was confident his methods would work. He had so much belief in himself and was convinced that he'd get us out of the league, even though it was starting to look like we were heading for the play-offs.

* * *

We were always playing catch-up after losing 4–2 at home to Reading at the end of March. That was a bad afternoon. Coley put us 1–0 up and we dominated the first half, only to find ourselves 2–1 down at the break. It was tough to take. Our normal defensive discipline wasn't there and the defeat meant that our chances of automatic promotion were fading.

Southampton and Reading were starting to pull away,

and we had too much to do during the run-in. It was our fault. The race went to the final day but the mood was flat when we closed our league campaign with a 2–1 victory over Hull at Upton Park. We should have been more ruthless and we were gutted after finishing third, two points below Southampton and three below Reading.

The frustrating thing was that we'd lost the fewest games in the division. The problem was drawing 14 games. We knew we'd need to be more clinical in order to avoid more complications in the play-offs.

On the bright side, Sam had hit upon a settled team. Ricardo Vaz Tê had scored loads of goals after joining us from Barnsley in January and Gary O'Neil, who was a tidy midfielder, had given us balance after returning from a broken ankle. We were enjoying a good run of form, and although teams who finish third often find it difficult to get over the disappointment of missing out on automatic promotion, I saw no signs of negativity in our dressing room before our semi-final against Cardiff.

Our confidence wasn't misplaced. We were better than Cardiff and proved it by winning the first leg 2–0 at their place. There was none of the usual play-off drama. Cardiff couldn't live with us and we did a professional job on them, two first-half goals from Jack silencing the Welsh crowd and giving us a healthy lead to take back to Upton Park.

Wins like that give you a natural high. It was late when we got back to Celtic Manor Resort, where we'd been booked in for an overnight stay in Newport, but we were too wired to go to sleep. We needed a way to blow off some steam, and me, Jack and Tonks all knew what to do when we saw the baskets of fruit in our rooms and remembered that there was a putting green outside the hotel.

It wasn't long before the three of us had invented the game of fruit golf. The rules were simple: we put a bit of money down, went out to the balcony with a few oranges and started trying to lob them into the holes out on the green.

We were just having a laugh. I chucked one out into the darkness, saw it bounce off the grass and watched it roll towards the target, only for a row to break out when the orange got stuck between the flag and the hole.

Did it count? Was it a hole-in-one? The others insisted I'd missed, even though the orange was clearly too big to fit inside, so I went down with Jack for an inspection.

We wiped the juice off the green and I thought nothing more of it after throwing the orange back to Tonks, who was watching us from the balcony. The argument was over, we were having some banter and the next thing I saw was Jack hitting the deck.

'What the f**k's happened here?' I wondered, peering down to check he wasn't hurt. I saw that Jack's face was dripping with orange juice – he looked ridiculous. There was orange peel everywhere and when I looked up I realised that he'd been taken out by an unwitting assailant.

Tonks didn't have a clue that he'd almost knocked Jack out. It was pitch black when he threw the orange off the balcony, and I was crying with laughter when we got back to the room. Even Jack saw the funny side once he stopped raging at Tonks and simmered down.

We were a tightknit group and we knew how to enjoy ourselves. The club was close to getting back on track and we secured our place at Wembley in style, thumping Cardiff 3–0 at Upton Park in the second leg.

We were almost there. The team was settled and Sam kept it quite chilled as we prepared to face Blackpool in the final. He gave us a few days off after the semi-final and the mood at training was positive. Nobody underestimated the size of the game. Nobody needed to tell us that it was one of the most important moments in West Ham's history.

We knew that it was going to be tough. Finals are never easy and Blackpool, who had come down with us the previous season, were an awkward side. They had plenty of good players and their manager, Ian Holloway, always sent them out to put on a show.

If anything, though, we were too confident when we arrived at Wembley. We'd beaten Blackpool 4–0 and 4–1 in the league, and most people thought we were nailed on to beat them easily again. They couldn't have been more wrong. Blackpool flew at us during the first 15 minutes, created a few chances and let us off the hook with some wasteful finishing.

We had to use our experience to stay in the game. Blackpool's young winger, Tom Ince, was causing problems and we needed to shut him down. After 34 minutes I went over to the left flank to challenge him, with Gary O'Neil and Matty Taylor getting stuck in too. We managed to get the ball away from him and when it ran to Matty he used his left foot to cross for Coley, who gave us the lead with a really clinical finish.

It seemed we were on the way. Yet it was back to square one when Ince equalised at the start of the second half. We went through a rocky spell and were lucky not to go 2–1 down.

Yet I always felt that we'd do it. Sam helped us regain our composure by making some good substitutions, changing his full-backs and bringing on Julien Faubert and George McCartney, and I was sure that we wouldn't concede again if we could find another goal from somewhere.

All eyes were on our forwards. Kev went close, smacking the bar with a volley. Then, with three minutes left, he went on a run down the left and sent a hopeful cross into the area. Coley challenged for it with the Blackpool defenders, the ball broke loose and Ricardo Vaz Tê became a West Ham legend when he smashed his shot into the top corner from six yards out.

Now it was time to concentrate. Blackpool didn't have long left and we just had to avoid doing anything stupid. Their only hope of an equaliser was if we made a mistake, so me and Kev absolutely ripped into Jack when he lost the ball in a dangerous area in midfield during stoppage time. 'Just f**king get rid of it!' Kev yelled. 'F**king hell,' Jack said after the final whistle. 'All I could hear was you two screaming at me.'

Emotions were running high. Winning promotion was so important and we couldn't afford to blow it. We couldn't take another year in the Championship. Hiring Sam had paid off. It wasn't pretty but the end had justified the means, and I didn't hear anyone complaining about the quality of our football when we were dancing around with the trophy at Wembley.

* * *

The only problem for me that was that I couldn't hang around for the after-party. My wedding was six days away and I'd already told Sam that I was booked to go to Dubai for my stag do straight after the final.

'Boss, I'm getting married on the 25th of May,' I said. 'I'm going to order some of them Virgin courier bikes to be at Wembley after the game to take me straight to Heathrow. I know we're supposed to have a party, but I can't organise it.'

It was a good job we won the game. Imagine how it would have felt if I'd gone on my stag after losing at Wembley or what my family would have been like at the wedding. It would have been horrendous after working so hard to get promoted.

But there was no need to worry. We were back in the Premier League and I was having the time of my life. I had a great few days with my mates and couldn't wait to get married to Carly at long last.

We had to be patient. We'd been engaged for 18 months and had planned to have the wedding at an earlier date, but Carly's granddad had been unwell and she wanted him to walk her down the aisle.

'Look, babe,' I'd said. 'I've got football to worry about and I need to get us promoted, so I'm happy to get married next year. Not a problem. But you're going to have to deal with it all.'

Carly took it in her stride. She was incredible. She picked Kew Gardens as our venue, got help from her cousin and her sister, and made sure that I didn't have to think about anything other than sorting out my suit. I didn't even know what food we were serving at the reception.

My job was simple: look smart and be on time. The one thing I love about it all is that I saw Carly in the lounge after the play-off final, gave her a kiss and a cuddle, and then jumped on the bike to get to the airport for Dubai. I didn't see her again before our wedding day. I had my back to everyone and I only turned around when Robert, who's one of my oldest friends, saw Carly walking down the aisle. 'F**king hell,' he said. 'She looks unbelievable.'

I couldn't wait. I swivelled round for a look. My little boy Lenny was all scruffy and my daughter Honey was crying her eyes out. But Carly looked amazing. I was lost for words when I saw her. We've been together since we were 14 and I know I wouldn't have had as good a career without her love and support.

Carly's been with me every step of the way. Obviously I couldn't stop crying during my speech. I was blown away by how beautiful our mums and sisters looked. I get emotional when I talk about the people I love. But I was at peace. I remember the room going silent when Dad stood up to make his speech and started it by saying, 'Mark signed a contract today.'

'F**king liar,' I thought. 'No I haven't.'

But on he went. 'It's the best contract he's ever going to sign in his life. And that's marrying Carly.'

It was a beautiful moment. There's nothing better than being surrounded by the people who mean the most to you in the world. I've never lost touch with my roots. Most of my mates have known me for ever and it means a lot that we've managed to stay close. They've never treated me like I'm something special, and they never miss a chance to hammer me. I'm just one of the lads to them.

I'm no different to anyone else. We were blown away when we went to the Maldives for our honeymoon. Neither of us had loads of money when we were kids, and being in a place as beautiful as that made me think about how lucky I was to play for West Ham.

I'd experienced so many ups and downs. I'd come through the academy, won promotion and played my part in our great escape in 2007. I'd come crashing back down to earth after three years of worrying about relegation and whether the club was going to survive. Now I was back on top of the world. West Ham were back in the Premier League, I'd just got married and I was in the Maldives with the love of my life. It was time for a moment of reflection. My mind went back to the start of my career and I thought about a piece of advice from Teddy Sheringham.

'Make sure you enjoy the good times,' he'd said. 'There's not many of them.'

7

Back Where We Belong

couldn't wait to play in the Premier League again. I felt fitter than ever after coming back from our honeymoon. One of the staff members at our hotel was on my case as soon as we landed in the Maldives. 'Mark,' he said, 'you play football. Do you want to come and play with us?'

'Mate, I'm on my honeymoon,' I said. 'I can't just run off and play football with you.'

I knew I had to be on my best behaviour with Carly. I was gagging to play, though, and the lad came back to ask me again the next day. 'Babe,' I said, turning to Carly, 'do you mind?'

Carly wasn't bothered. I headed off into the staff quarters, where they had a brand spanking new five-a-side pitch with mini goals at either end, and I spent a few hours there every day. The standard was pretty good and the heat meant I was in great condition by the time we flew back to London.

I was raring to go before the start of the season. I wasn't worried about our ability to compete in the Premier League. We had a strong side, and I was convinced that Sam was going to bring in players who knew the league and would be able to carry out his instructions.

Sam had been there and done it. Nothing was going to knock him off course, and his summer recruitment was spot on. He didn't have huge sums of money, but there was a purpose to every signing. He brought in Jussi Jääskeläinen to be his No1 after losing Greeno on a free. Yossi Benayoun, who was still technically brilliant, came in on loan from Chelsea, and signing Mo Diamé from Wigan was a masterstroke. You couldn't hold on to the ball for too long when Mo was around. He helped my game a lot. I could get around the pitch, but I was nowhere near as quick or strong as Mo, whose ball-winning abilities meant I had room to pick my passes and Kev had even more freedom to drive into the box.

We struck up a good balance in midfield, and we were backed up with a solid defence. Tonks and Winston had made huge strides, and I was delighted when Sam asked me to help him out by convincing James Collins to come back to the club.

I was straight on the phone. 'Ginge, the gaffer won't stop talking to me about you,' I said. 'You've got to come back.'

'Well, tell him to put a f**king bid in then!' Ginge said.

I'd done my bit. Ginge was desperate to return and he was back at Upton Park in time for our opening game. We were at home to Aston Villa, Ginge's former club, and although it wasn't a classic, we never looked like losing and we grabbed all the points when Ricardo Vaz Tê set up Kev to score the winner just before half-time.

We didn't look like a team in danger of going down. Sam didn't dwell on our 3–0 defeat against Swansea that followed as he was too busy trying to sign Andy Carroll on loan from Liverpool. He was absolutely obsessed with Andy, and it was a huge boost when we managed to get the deal done in time for the big man to start up front when we hosted Fulham at the end of August.

It was a game-changer of a signing. Andy was so dominant in the air and he instantly became a fan favourite after helping us beat Fulham 3–0 on his debut. 'He's much better than I realised,' I thought, watching how easily Andy controlled the ball on his chest and brought others into play. It wasn't hard to work out why Sam wanted him so badly. Defenders hated trying to challenge Andy when we hit the ball long and his arrival brought the best out of Kev, who loved feeding off his knock-downs and lay-offs.

Those two had such a clever partnership. Andy was involved when Kev volleyed us into an early lead against Fulham, who couldn't live with our aerial power, and it was exciting to think about Matt Jarvis swinging in crosses for both of them from the left wing.

Jarvo was another shrewd signing. Sam wanted someone to deliver for Andy and Kev, and I really enjoyed playing with Jarvo. He was so quick and he always tried to run behind his full-back. It made my life easier because Sam was still moaning at me for not knocking the ball in behind enough.

'Listen,' I said. 'I'm only going to do it if someone's running there. I'm not going to just play it in behind to no one.'

'Yeah, but put it there and something will happen,' Sam said. 'Just you watch.'

I felt more comfortable with Jarvo because I knew he'd be on the move if I played the pass. We were building a decent side, and while we had a few disappointing results at times we fancied our chances of causing an upset when Chelsea came to Upton Park at the start of December.

There were, however, a couple of concerns before the game. Andy was out for a couple of months with a knee injury and I wasn't sure when Sam decided to try Tonks in

midfield during training. I understood that Sam was looking for a way to make us more secure in the middle and I
knew that Tonks was good technically. But he wasn't a
natural in midfield, he wasn't used to dealing with all the
movement around him and we had to shelve the experi-
ment at half-time.

Eden Hazard and Juan Mata had given us the runa-
round and Chelsea should have been more than 1–0 up.
Yet we were still in the game. The only way was up and
Sam reacted decisively during the break, putting Tonks out
of his misery and forcing Chelsea back by bringing Mo off
the bench.

Mo's energy changed the game. We got on top of
Chelsea and they couldn't find a way out of their half. The
pressure was relentless. Coley equalised after an hour, Mo
sent Upton Park wild by firing us into the lead with four
minutes left and the points were ours when a counterattack ended with Modibo Maïga making it 3–1.

It was a memorable win, our first over Chelsea in almost
a decade, though Tonks was still stewing on his performance after the game. He couldn't understand how I
managed to survive in midfield every week, and he wasn't
in a rush to go through that experience again.

But that was Sam – he was always thinking outside the
box. I had my own opinions about our tactics and I used
to go with Kev to have loads of chats with Sam about the

team. Ultimately, though, managers have to trust their own instincts. Sam didn't care what people thought. He was surrounded by a solid backroom team – he trusted his assistant, Neil McDonald, and our goalkeeping coach, Martyn Margetson, who went on to join the England set-up – and he was prepared to take the flak if a plan backfired. Sam wasn't bothered about criticism. He had too much self-belief to let it affect him.

*   *   *

Nothing ever stopped Sam from following his own path. His ideas came off more often than not and the team was built in his image. We never worried about a lack of organisation. We didn't see much of Sam at the training ground on a Monday or Tuesday, but Thursday and Friday were his days. He worked tirelessly with the defence and always brought some kids over to help us with our shape.

It wasn't always enjoyable. I found some games difficult under Sam, just as there were times I wasn't happy under Avram, Curbs, Gianfranco and Pards. But the constant complaints about us being dull and negative didn't register with me. Football's only enjoyable when you win. There were times in my career when I played well against a big team and received no praise because we lost. On the other hand, there were times when I had a right stinker and people would come up and say, 'Well done, you were great today' because we won 3–0.

It's difficult to take the outside noise seriously. Winning is all that counts and only real football people know when you've played well. Football's a game of opinions, but there were times when I looked at a newspaper and thought, 'How can someone give me 5 out of 10 when I was the best player on the pitch?'

I never understood how a reporter could comment with absolute certainty on a player's performance. I'd never pass judgement on a doctor's work. I don't know what it's like to operate on a human body, just like fans and journalists have no idea how hard it is to carve out a successful career in the Premier League.

Over time I stopped paying attention to my critics and I learnt to bite my tongue. I knew it wouldn't have done anyone any good if I'd gone on Twitter to have a pop at a journalist I didn't like: 'He's the worst journalist I've ever seen. He's shit. His reports are shit. He hasn't got a clue what he's talking about.'

That's the kind of thing people say about footballers. You go on social media and see people saying, 'He's shit … he shouldn't play … why's he in the team?' and you just think, 'Why don't you come and give it a go if you think it's so easy?'

I ended up losing patience with my mate Robert. He plays in goal at Sunday League level and has spent the last 25 years talking to me about the art of goalkeeping. We'd sit around a table having a beer and I'd listen to him slagging off professional keepers.

'He's shit.'

'Mate, he's probably not shit. He plays in the Premier League.'

It drove me mad, so I came up with a plan when I was on holiday with him and a few mates in Dubai. I knew Marge, our goalkeeping coach, was out there too, and he agreed to come along when I asked him to join us on a night out.

I knew what was going to happen. It was a lovely evening, but Rob wouldn't stop talking about keepers and Marge eventually decided to teach him a lesson. 'I'll tell you what, Rob,' he said. 'When we're safe at the end of the season, come in and train with the first team. I'll give you a session and then the boys can do some shooting at you after.'

Rob should have realised it was a trap. 'Listen to me,' I said. 'I hope you never slag off a goalie again after what happens to you when you come in.'

But Rob just palmed me off. He came to training and Marge, who has one of the hardest half-volleys I've ever seen on a goalkeeping coach, gave him a full-blown session. It was a proper pounding and Rob was so far off the pace.

He was dripping with sweat by the time we got to him and started taking shots

It wasn't a contest. Rob was diving after the ball had already hit the back of the net and he was an absolute state when we got back to the car. He called his dad and his hands were shaking because he'd used his muscles so much. 'I'll never, ever, ever slag off a goalkeeper again in my life,' he told me. 'I cannot believe how hard you hit the ball and how accurate you are.'

It was just a way of making Rob think twice about sitting around and criticising Premier League goalkeepers. But these days a lot of journalists and kids on social media get drawn to shiny things. Not everyone can be a Kevin De Bruyne or a Lionel Messi. But people see one piece of skill on YouTube and think a player's a superstar. It's happened loads at West Ham – I've seen fans go mad over players who do a couple of stepovers and put a nice cross in, ignoring the fact that they make the team weaker because they never track back to cover their left-back.

There's a difference between what fans see and what actually helps a team become successful. I hope Chelsea and England fans appreciate the value of a player as diligent as Mason Mount. It's clear to see why Frank Lampard and Thomas Tuchel relied on him so much at Chelsea, and why he's become such an important part of Gareth Southgate's England team.

Mason Mount has everything you'd want in a midfielder. He doesn't do loads of tricks, so people criticise him for not being a flair player, but he scores goals, gets assists and works incredibly hard. Why wouldn't Southgate play him?

People think there's always something better waiting just round the corner. I had that issue throughout my career. At West Ham a lot of fans decided that they were bored with me putting in consistent, unfussy performances all the time. They thought I needed to be replaced. They were drawn to the idea of something different, just like Carly will look around our front room and decide that it's been too long since we changed our wallpaper.

It was similar for Sam. He found us in a horrendous mess, took us up and established us in the Premier League. There was nothing wrong with his football as far as I was concerned.

* * *

I never, ever felt like we were in danger of getting relegated under Sam. Our first season after promotion passed by without much drama. We had a settled, committed side and the next step for Sam was working out how to inject a bit more quality into the squad.

I was thrilled that Joe Cole, whose career had stalled at Liverpool, agreed to come back to the club at the start of

January. I didn't know Joe that well but he was my hero when I was coming through the academy. It was devastating when relegation forced us to sell him to Chelsea in 2003. Joe went on to bigger and better things at Chelsea and, having been invited to Stamford Bridge to watch him in a couple of Champions League games, I couldn't wait to play in the same team as him.

Upton Park was rocking for Joe's second West Ham debut – a glamorous FA Cup third-round tie against Manchester United. He inspired us after we went 1–0 down early on. He swung in a couple of crosses for Ginge to put us 2–1 up and United needed a stunning last-minute equaliser from Robin van Persie to earn a replay, which we lost 1–0.

It was great to have Joe around. I gained more than a solid team-mate; I gained a proper friend. I have so much respect for the guy. He played at the highest level for ages and could have hung up his boots after leaving West Ham on a free transfer at the end of the 2013–14 season. Instead, he gave it a go at Aston Villa before dropping down to League One to play for Coventry City, and he ended his career by moving to the States to play for Tampa Bay Rowdies.

I don't know if I could have been as adventurous as Joe. He was so enthusiastic and his passion for the game was ridiculous. He just wanted a ball, a pitch and a pair of boots. 'I've got to take my hat off to him,' I thought when I saw Joe playing in America. 'He could easily have just sat around and stopped, but it's unreal how he's still going.'

Joe's love of football was enormous and it was just a shame that he couldn't make more of a success of his return to West Ham. There were a few promising moments, evidence that his natural talent was still there, but the problem was that Joe couldn't trust his body any more. He kept getting injured and we didn't see enough of him.

Sam needed attacking reinforcements if we were going to push on after finishing the 2012–13 season in 10th place. We managed to keep Andy, making his loan permanent for £15m, and our business with Liverpool wasn't done yet. Sam also had his eye on Stewart Downing, who was a top winger, and I was delighted when we signed him. I'd seen Stewy have loads of good games against us, he settled in well with the lads and he knew the league inside out.

It seemed that Sam had a plan: a solid defence, an organised midfield, and Jarvo and Stewy swinging crosses into the box for Andy and Kev. Yet the 2013–14 season turned into a year of frustration. A persistent foot injury kept Andy out for ages and, without him leading the line, the goals dried up. I felt for Sam. His options were limited – Modibo Maïga was proving an unsuitable understudy for Andy – and he'd already spent the summer budget. It was simply a case of bringing in anyone who was available, and as we were hunting for bargains we ended up going for Mladen Petrić on a free transfer and re-signing Coley, who'd left us on a free a few months earlier.

In those circumstances it wasn't a surprise that our form dipped and we slid down the table. We couldn't score, and, after starting the season with one win from our first six games, Sam decided that he needed an alternative approach when we visited Spurs at the start of October. 'Right, you f**kers,' he said when we arrived for training on Friday morning, 'we're going to try something on Sunday, but no one f**king tell anyone what we're going to do. We're not going to play a striker. We're just going to play a midfield four with two wingers.'

None of us saw it coming. But nor did Spurs. They didn't know what was going on. We were solid, hit them on the counterattack and deservedly went ahead when Winston bundled in a corner at the start of the second half.

There was no response from Spurs. A few minutes later I won the ball in midfield, did a bit of skill to buy myself some space and sent Ricardo Vaz Tê through on goal. Ricardo made it 2–0, though I didn't get an assist because he tried to score with a nutty stepover and was lucky that the ball rebounded in off him after his initial effort was saved by Hugo Lloris.

I didn't care, though. We were on our way to our first win at Spurs since 1999 and our third goal is one that has gone down in West Ham folklore.

Everyone remembers Ravel Morrison taking the piss at White Hart Lane. He'd joined us from Manchester United 18 months earlier and had proven himself after Sam sent him on loan to Birmingham. It seemed that Rav was ready to make the step up and we all watched in awe as he ran rings around Spurs, dancing past a host of defenders before dinking the ball over Lloris to make it 3–0.

The fans had a new hero. They fell in love with Rav because of his magic touch and for a while it seemed that we had a future star on our hands. Rav had the world at his feet. The question was what he was going to make of the opportunity that Sam had given him.

* * *

There was no doubt that Rav had the tools to become a top player. The quality of his performances in pre-season was a joke after he came back from Birmingham. He had an unreal game when we played a friendly against Oxford, and me and Kev spent the entire coach journey home trying to convince him not to waste his potential. 'You can really help us out this year,' I said. 'Just get your head down, concentrate and you can become a f**king top player for us.'

Rav made out that he was taking our advice on board. He promised us that he was going to try his hardest. He insisted that he was going to knuckle down. Then he went back up north and didn't come into training for four days.

It was sad to watch Rav make one bad choice after another. Sam's man-management was excellent and he spent a lot of time trying to get Rav to put the work in to becoming a team player. That was Sam's only demand. He knew this kid was on a different level to the rest of us and although Rav made mistakes at times, I couldn't help but love him.

I felt genuinely affectionate towards him. He was ridiculous at training and his cheek always made me laugh. He'd slip the ball through my legs, then celebrate by looking at me and raising his eyebrows up and down, as if he was saying, 'You see that?'

Obviously I tried to boot his legs off in response. Obviously Rav was too quick for me. He moved with the ball so easily and could glide past players like they weren't there. Rav's talent was unreal and I'm grateful that West Ham fans saw him at his best for six months. His goal against Spurs will never be forgotten, and there was also a game against Fulham where he came off the bench for a 25-minute cameo and stole the show by nutmegging three defenders in a row.

There was an innocence to Rav. We knew something was up when he brought two suitcases on a mid-season trip to Dubai. We opened up the second one and were baffled to find it was full of Pot Noodles, tins of tuna and jars of mayonnaise. 'I didn't think I'd like the food out here,' Rav said. We just laughed. The food in Dubai is incredible, but he stuck to his own menu. He was such a funny character.

Yet it wasn't sustainable. I was aware that he'd had a tough upbringing and had left United because of issues off the pitch. Ultimately his mentality wasn't good enough, though I never judged him. Everyone expects footballers to be robots but we all have problems. Football was probably a way for Rav to deal with the challenges he faced when he was growing up. There's no point saying that he should have behaved more professionally. We're all wired in different ways and I think that he struggled with living so far away from home.

I tried to be understanding with Rav and I knew he wouldn't turn up at times. He was supposed to be in the squad when we hosted Arsenal on Boxing Day, but he had other ideas. We were waiting for him at the stadium on Christmas Day and only realised that Rav wasn't going to join us when he posted a picture on Instagram of him and his family up north.

It was inevitable that Sam eventually decided that he couldn't rely on him. We'd been sucked into a relegation fight and kept losing players to injury. All of our centre-backs were out at one stage, forcing Sam to bring Roger Johnson in as an emergency loan, and we were desperate for Andy to recover from his injury.

Goals were still a problem. We had no luck. Modibo came up with an unforgettable moment, scoring the winner when we fought back from a goal down at White Hart Lane and won our League Cup quarter-final against Spurs, but we drew Manchester City in the last four and they walloped us 9–0 on aggregate.

Sam had to go back to basics. He brought in a couple of Italian lads on loan, Antonio Nocerino and Marco Borriello, and we had a solid core. If we lost a game I'd sit down with Kev in the morning, have a cup of tea and tell him that we needed to rattle a few cages in training. 'Right,' I'd say, 'we've got to get these boys out there today and have a right go in training.'

We needed the lads to know that there was nothing more important than the next game. We could rely on our organisation and we were delighted when a battling defensive display earned us a 0–0 draw with Chelsea at the end of January. Adrián, our new Spanish goalkeeper, was unbeatable, and it was music to Sam's ears when José Mourinho accused us of using 19th-century tactics. Sam loved knowing that he'd got under José's skin. He relished winding people up and wasn't the slightest bit bothered about people criticising him for sending his side out to defend.

Sam always put the result first and he knew how to make the most of the tools at his disposal. If we'd not had him to give the team a proper structure we probably would have gone down. We had so many injuries and the season could easily have ended in disaster under a different manager.

Yet there was a lack of appreciation for Sam's efforts from the fans. While Andy's return from injury in January lifted us, a run of three consecutive defeats in March put us under pressure before a must-win game against Hull. They went down to 10 men in the first half and I gave us the lead with a penalty, but we didn't play well. We only won 2–1, the Upton Park crowd greeting the full-time whistle with loud boos and Sam responding by cupping his ears at them.

It was horrible and Sam couldn't believe the reaction. We were never going to open up and play like Real Madrid against Hull. We played badly, we got the win and we moved on. All that mattered at that stage was making sure we survived. You can't worry about playing fancy football when you're in a scrap. You've got to roll up your sleeves, dig in and make sure you're not in the bottom three come the end of the season.

Yet the fans had different priorities. They wanted more excitement, and patience was wearing thin on both sides.

The culture at West Ham is demanding. The club's reputation as the 'Academy of Football' is difficult for any manager to live up to, but the growing complaints about a lack of entertainment made no sense to Sam. His view was that he'd done his job when we finished 13th, even though the season wasn't going to live long in anyone's memory, and the constant debate as to whether or not he played football the 'West Ham way' was beginning to become an unwanted distraction.

*   *   *

Sam didn't have much time for the 'West Ham way'. He scoffed at it when he arrived in 2011, pointing out that the club had spent the last three years losing, and to be honest I don't really know where the phrase comes from. I don't agree with the idea that it's about playing good football and keeping the ball on the floor. There's more to being successful than trying to be entertaining. Look at the West Ham team that went down in 2003 – they had Paolo Di Canio, Trevor Sinclair, Joe Cole, Michael Carrick, Freddie Kanouté, Jermain Defoe, David James and Glen Johnson, but they failed. Something went wrong, they couldn't sort it out in time and the club experienced a devastating relegation.

It's why simply finding a way to win means everything to a footballer. We played good football under Gianfranco, but the fans weren't happy because we lost all the time. We ended up in the Championship and needed Sam to get us up.

My view is that the 'West Ham way' means hard work, honesty and aggression. I always told new players that the fans would welcome them with open arms if they saw them playing for the badge. 'Give it everything you've got,' I said. 'If it's not good enough, they'll accept that.'

It's great playing fantastic, winning football. Yet it isn't always possible. The problem is that fans have been brain-washed into thinking that every manager has to emulate Pep Guardiola. We've been blessed to watch his teams over the last 15 years and, because Pep had such a big influence on English football, managers who don't use a high line and ask their defenders to play out from the back are derided as negative dinosaurs.

My argument is that it's harder to take risks if you don't have the best players. I don't think a manager is doing his job correctly if he isn't playing to his team's strengths. I was baffled when I saw a League One team attempt to take City on at their own game recently. They tried to pass the ball around their own area and ended up conceding three cheap goals in the biggest game of their lives.

Admittedly it's a tricky balancing act. Do you praise the coach for sticking to his beliefs? Or do you question why he didn't tell his team to remove the element of risk and give themselves a chance of beating City by getting the ball up the other end of the pitch?

We all see the game in different ways and I accept that there isn't necessarily a right answer. Yet it's interesting that Liverpool, who play wonderful football under Jürgen Klopp, can be extremely direct. At West Ham I want academy players to be honest, show respect, work hard and listen to their coaches. Nowhere does it say that a young player can't hit a long ball. It isn't realistic. The majority of players just want to be given the best possible chance of winning a game.

All the same it was clear that Sam had to look at evolving our style before the 2014–15 season. He wasn't popular with the fans, he'd a year left on his contract and the board had considered making a change during the summer. The clock had started ticking.

Sam, however, would argue that he just needed to sign more technical players. He had Youri Djorkaeff, Nicolas Anelka and Jay-Jay Okocha when he was in charge of Bolton, and he was slowly building a more expansive side at West Ham. Stewy Downing was so intelligent on the ball and our midfield went up a level when Sam pulled off the signing of Alex Song on loan from Barcelona.

Song was unbelievable during the first half of the season. We'd got off to a slow start, losing two of our first three games, but the new boys were a breath of fresh air.

Aaron Cresswell and Carl Jenkinson were clever additions in the full-back positions, Cheikhou Kouyaté made our midfield more powerful, Mauro Zárate offered a bit of unpredictability, Diafra Sakho and Enner Valencia were exciting additions up front, and I quickly realised why Song had played at the highest level for Arsenal and Barcelona.

It said a lot for Sam's recruitment skills that we managed to cope with Andy and Kev both out injured. There were positive signs when we drew 2–2 with Hull – Enner scored a banger from 30 yards and Sakho secured us a point – and we caused a bit of a stir when we hosted Liverpool in our next game. Enner and Sakho terrorised their defence with their pace and movement, me, Cheikhou and Song absolutely dominated midfield, and Stewy was outstanding after being moved into a free role by Sam.

The fans couldn't believe what they were watching. We swept into a 2–0 lead inside the first seven minutes and we held our nerve after Liverpool pulled one back. We didn't panic when Stevie Gerrard, who was playing in a deeper role under Brendan Rodgers, started to spray a few passes around. Sam called me over to ask me to stop Stevie during the final 30 minutes, but I had a different idea.

'Boss, just put Stewy on Stevie G,' I said. 'We'll work midfield for the final half-hour – just tell Stewy to stand on Stevie so he can't get the ball.'

The plan worked a treat. Me, Song and Cheikhou sat back, and I told Stewy not to worry about tracking back to help us out. 'Just leave me be,' I said. 'You concentrate on stopping Stevie G.' Stewy didn't argue. He stuck to Stevie and negated his influence on the game, taking away most of Liverpool's threat. They never looked like equalising and we sealed a massive win when Stewy set up Morgan Amalfitano to make it 3–1.

Nobody saw it coming. We'd beaten a big side in style, and when I looked back on my discussion with Sam about how to stop Stevie I realised that I could become a better player by being more tactical. It struck me that I could influence a game by evaluating it from the inside, speaking to the manager and working out a strategy that would give us a better chance of victory.

I was maturing. I was evolving my game, my self-doubt and hunger to improve always driving me on, and it was enjoyable to see how quickly we were developing as a team. We went on an unbelievable run and caught a lot of people by surprise. We were fourth at Christmas, Champions League qualification was a genuine possibility and the fans were starting to modify their views on Sam. The mood at the club changed. There were no complaints about our football any more.

*   *   *

The vibes were good before we went to play Chelsea on Boxing Day, although Sam wasn't in my good books at the time. I'd taken one for the team by playing with an Achilles injury when we beat Newcastle 1–0 at the end of November and I was livid when Sam left me out against West Brom three days later. 'I played with an injury because we were short of players,' I thought. 'Why the f**k did I put my body through that? I helped him out and could have hurt myself badly.'

I couldn't understand it. I flew into Sam's office after training and sent a stream of expletives his way. I wasn't looking at the situation through his eyes, but being honest I was in no condition to play. The Achilles kept me out of action for a month and I was still miles off the pace when Sam decided that my first game back would be Chelsea away.

I was like a lamb to the slaughter. Chelsea were on course to win the league under José Mourinho and they were far too strong for us. It was the first time I'd played against Diego Costa, whose technique was incredible, and I couldn't get near Cesc Fàbregas in midfield. Cesc was a phenomenal player, one of the best the Premier League has ever seen. I had some great battles and arguments with him down the years, and although he was better than me I enjoyed watching him up close and learning from how he played.

I liked testing myself against the very best, although it's impossible when they're on form. Teams like West Ham only have a chance against teams such as City, United and Chelsea if they have an off day and we play to our absolute maximum. But if they work hard and apply themselves properly it's a demoralising experience.

It was like that against José's Chelsea. We were lucky it only finished 2–0. They absolutely dominated us and Eden Hazard was extraordinary. I was just buzzing I didn't have to mark him. Hazard was frightening when he was on it. He was so balanced on the ball and he made life miserable for our full-backs, tormenting Cress in the first half before switching to the opposite flank to run at Jenko after half-time. 'Mate, he's an absolute scandal,' Cress said after the game. 'He's the best player I've ever played in my life.'

It was a reality check for all of us and our top-four challenge took another dent when we lost at home to Arsenal two days later. Our momentum had stalled. Sam was out of contract at the end of the season and it seemed that the owners had already decided to make a change. Sam's motivation drained away once he realised that a new deal wasn't coming his way.

The frustration was that we were still in a good position after the Christmas period. We were still in the hunt for fourth and Upton Park was bouncing after we reached the fourth round of the FA Cup thanks to a memorable victory over Everton. The tie was full of drama and Adrián, our goalkeeper, was the hero when the replay went to a penalty shootout. It was ridiculous when he whipped off his gloves before scoring the winning penalty.

It seemed, briefly, that we were set for a cup run. But everything went wrong when we visited West Brom in the fifth round. I was so unwell when we travelled up on the coach on the day before the game that I was convinced I was going to shit myself. Somehow I survived until we got to the hotel, but I couldn't get off the toilet before dinner. I staggered downstairs, asked the doctor for some Imodium and took four at once because I was so desperate to make sure I was ready to play.

I ought to have known better. I didn't tell the doctor how bad I felt and I was the biggest bag of shit the next day. The tablets didn't kick in until 3 a.m. and I should have told Sam that I'd been up all night. Instead I stayed quiet, pretended I was fine and played like an absolute idiot. What was I trying to prove? I ended up putting in one of the worst performances of my career and I was furious with myself after West Brom destroyed our cup dream, thrashing us 4–0. 'Why do you do that to yourself?' I thought. 'Why don't you just say, "I'm not well"?'

My determination to play at all costs caught up with me. Nobody can argue with a hamstring strain, but you fear you won't be taken seriously if you say you're too unwell to play. I was too embarrassed to say that I had the shits, and I was so worried about someone coming in and taking my place that I didn't realise I was in no condition to help the team.

That said, it probably wouldn't have made a big difference if I'd pulled out. The humiliation against West Brom showed how badly our season was running out of steam. Sam had switched off because of the lack of signings and the uncertainty over his future inevitably affected our form.

It was frustrating for the players because club policy lay outside of our control. We couldn't understand why Nenê, an ageing Brazilian winger who'd been playing in the Middle East, was our only signing during January. We were stuck in the middle, caught between Sam and the board, and we never looked capable of rediscovering our spark.

Song's decline didn't help. He was quite a casual player, the kind of character who'd jog out to train with his tracksuit bottoms pulled down low, and Sam lost patience with him when we stopped winning. It wasn't a healthy situation, although the breakdown of Sam's relationship with Song was far from our only problem. We won just three league games after Christmas and our performance against Newcastle on the final day summed up our malaise.

They needed to win to stay up and they couldn't have asked for more obliging opponents than us.

There was no surprise when Sam's departure was confirmed after the game. He was content with the job he'd done and I was sad to see him go, but the season had fizzled out, the fans were disgruntled and we'd grown stale. The relationship had run its course. The time had come to try something new.

8

Farewell, Boleyn

Letting Sam go was a risky decision. He'd spent four years putting the squad together and we knew he'd keep us in the Premier League. Yet the owners were ready to take a leap of faith. They wanted to give the fans more entertainment and there was a lot of excitement when Slaven Bilić, who was a fan favourite for West Ham in the 90s, landed the job.

I was impressed when I met Slaven for the first time. He had so much charm, he wasn't afraid to lead and he backed himself to build on the foundations laid by Sam. Slav, who immediately came across as a good man and a talented coach, didn't try to do anything too revolutionary. He knew that he'd inherited a solid team from Sam. The defence was organised, the midfield worked hard and I felt that we'd have a chance of pushing on if we added more creativity in the final third.

Slav's first signing set the tone. Dimitri Payet, Marseille's gifted French winger, was the kind of player who got fans on their feet. We went to Ireland during pre-season and I fancied our chances of doing well when I saw Dimi train for the first time. He had magic in his boots, and I quickly saw why Slav wanted to build the team round him.

Dimi's status as our main man wasn't up for debate. Slav had made up his mind to use him as his No10, even though doing so meant stepping on Stewart Downing's toes. Middlesbrough were in for Stewy and, while I tried to convince him to stay, the opportunity to go back to his boyhood club was too good for him to turn down.

At least we well placed to cope with Stewy leaving. Along with signing Dimi, Slav was also set on bringing in a little Argentinian kid who was playing out in the Middle East. I couldn't believe my eyes when I saw Manuel Lanzini walk out for his first training session. He looked so tiny, and I was convinced he was going to struggle with the physicality of the Premier League.

But then the ball came to Manu. 'Oh my God,' I thought. 'We've got a player here.' Manu's technique was superb and he quickly hit it off with Dimi. They had a great understanding on the pitch and Slav had a way of making his creative players feel that they had freedom to express themselves on the pitch.

I was encouraged. 'We look a good team with Dimi,' I thought, though pre-season wasn't entirely smooth. Our performances were hit and miss, and our preparations were complicated by our attempts to qualify for the group stage of the Europa League. It was a weird situation. We'd qualified for the preliminary stages because of our Fair Play record, and having to go through a series of play-offs meant our schedule was unusually hectic, summed up by our season starting with a tie against Andorran side Lusitans on 2 July.

It was difficult for Slav to strike the right balance between getting us ready for the Premier League and making sure we could compete in Europe. He used a mix of first-team players and youngsters during the Europa League qualifiers and we didn't have much of a flow. We were playing competitive fixtures while we were still in pre-season mode and although we cruised past Lusitans we had a scare in the next round, almost crashing out when we travelled to Malta to face Birkirkara FC in testing conditions.

The pitch was awful, it was roasting hot and we were up against it when Tonks got sent off in the first half. We needed penalties to go through, but it was becoming a grind. Slav wasn't fussed about Europe. He knew that we weren't ready to play at that level. The squad wasn't deep enough and he was right to prioritise the league. We didn't need the distraction and nobody cared when our reserves lost to Astra Giurgiu in the third qualifying round.

Going out to Astra was a blessing in disguise. We were relieved not to have to think about Europe any more. The defeat allowed us to focus on our domestic form, and we were fully in the zone when we started our league campaign with a daunting trip to Arsenal on the opening weekend.

Nobody expected us to get us a result at the Emirates Stadium. Yet there was no hangover from our defeat to Astra three days earlier. We'd strengthened our defence by signing Angelo Ogbonna from Juventus and we were ready to give Arsenal a game. Slav's team-talk was so passionate and he set us up brilliantly, our counterattacking game working perfectly, our back four keeping Arsenal's forwards quiet and Dimi full of trickery whenever he got on the ball.

Dimi made us tick. He created chances, played with no fear and swung in a great free-kick for Cheikhou to head us into the lead on the stroke of half-time. It was no smash and grab. We didn't just sit back and defend for our lives. We were prepared to take risks on the ball, and the points were ours when Mauro Zárate banged one in from 25 yards at the start of the second half.

We were ecstatic after the game. We weren't quite sure what to expect after Sam's departure, and Slav was under a lot of pressure to keep us safe. It was our final season at Upton Park, so Slav didn't want to be responsible for taking us down before our move to the London Stadium. Beating Arsenal in such style suggested that we weren't going to be in a relegation battle. 'You know what,' I thought. 'We're actually going to do something special this year.'

* * *

We couldn't have dreamt of a better way to start the season. Everyone was raving about the new-look West Ham after our win over Arsenal, and we didn't expect to be given such a tough time when we hosted Leicester City a week later. I was surprised by how quick, strong and talented they were, and although we didn't play particularly badly, Dimi's first goal in claret and blue wasn't enough to save us from a disappointing 2–1 defeat.

It was a reminder that we weren't the finished article, and it was a difficult experience for our promising young defender Reece Oxford. There was loads of hype around Reece after he made his debut against Arsenal at the age of 16. He had an impressive game in defensive midfield, catching the eye by keeping Mesut Özil quiet, and everyone on the outside expected him to kick on and hit those levels every week.

Yet Reece was only a kid. The pressure on him was intense, reminding me of what I went through when I first broke into the team, and it was too much, too soon. Suddenly everyone wanted a piece of Reece – agents, rival teams, hanger-ons – and he struggled to handle it. His form dipped, he fell out of the team and he left a couple of years later.

The spotlight on Reece shone too brightly. Everyone got carried away and I'm glad that he's found his feet after going to Germany to learn his trade at FC Augsburg. He needed to get away from West Ham. He needed space to learn. People expected big things from Reece because he was already training with the first team when he was 15, but what they don't realise is that some youngsters stand out because they have a quicker physical development than others.

It doesn't mean they have the most talent and in Reece's case it's easy to forget that he didn't really know how to play in midfield. He'd made his name in the academy at centre-back and the reason he played well against Arsenal was because we didn't have much of the ball. Defending wasn't a problem for him. He held his position, intercepted passes and stuck to Özil, but that's not the same as taking the ball and getting the team on the move.

The Leicester game exposed Reece's limitations in midfield. The game passed him by and he was taken off at half-time, though he wasn't alone in struggling to handle Leicester's quality. They outplayed us in the first half, and we had another setback when we hosted newly promoted Bournemouth a week later, defending amateurishly and losing 4–3 in front of an exasperated Upton Park crowd.

'F**k me,' I thought. 'Not again.' I knew we had a good team, but the defeat to Bournemouth worried me. We were poor without the ball, gave away some silly goals and appeared to have lost the solidity that characterised us under Sam.

Yet Slav was confident in his approach. He was changing our style and was willing to move on some of Sam's stalwarts. Kevin Nolan wasn't really in Slav's plans, even though he was still captain, and he struck a deal with the owners to end his contract after being taken off at half-time during the Bournemouth game.

I was sad to see Kev go. Recently he told me that he should have given it a bit more time. 'I should have just done what you did in your last couple of years,' he said. 'I should have hung around the place and played on when I was needed. But I didn't really want to do that.'

It's a shame that Kev wasn't content with a bit-part role under Slav. He would have been a useful option off the bench when we needed a goal, and he was a proper leader.

Kev never shirked his responsibilities. He always laced his boots up and went out to play, even when things weren't going well for him on the pitch. His mentality was incredible. He got more stick than he deserved at times, but you could always trust him to turn up, and he had an unbelievable knack of going out there and scoring the winner.

I benefited so much from being around him. I was his vice-captain and I learnt from how well he shut out the noise. I made sure to take that on board. People expect the club captain to step up during challenging times, and Kev never let anything affect him. He was perfectly suited to the demands of the role and it was only when I replaced him that I realised there's far more to it than wearing the armband on a matchday.

I'd filled in for Kev at times, captaining the side for the first time when he missed a trip to Derby County on New Year's Day in 2012. Yet I tried not to forget my place. I'd always hand Kev the armband if I was playing and he'd come on as a substitute, just as Declan Rice did with me when I was approaching the end of my career. I thought it was important to respect the pecking order and I was furious with myself when I forgot to give Kev the armband after he came off the bench during our win over Arsenal.

In my defence there wasn't long left and I was totally focused on making sure that Arsenal didn't get back into the game. But it played on my mind and I ended up texting him an apology later that night.

'Kev, look,' I said. 'I'm so f**king sorry, mate. You came on today and I didn't give you the armband. It showed a lack of respect and I regret it.'

'Nobes, don't be f**king stupid,' Kev replied. 'You're mad. What are you on about?'

I should have left it there. But my forgetfulness still plays on my mind. I know I should have put it behind me by now, but it looked rubbish. I needed to be more responsible. You just go out and play when you're the vice-captain. The club captain has to think about representing the entire institution. You liaise with the manager, defend the team and know that you can never hide on the pitch.

That's how Kev did it and I knew I had big shoes to fill following his departure. It was a huge honour to take on the captaincy and I was determined to make a strong start, though the fixture computer wasn't on my side. We'd just suffered two bad home defeats and our next assignment was a trip to Liverpool. It seemed that things were about to get worse.

*　　*　　*

We hadn't won at Anfield since 1963. 'It's going to be tough up there,' Dad said, but I felt weirdly confident when we arrived on Merseyside. Training was sharp, we'd shown that we could score and the dressing room was bouncing before kick-off. Whoever was in charge of the pre-match music had chosen some Whitney Houston love songs, only for Slav to step in and get us in the zone by putting his nutty rock music on.

The change of tone worked a treat. We weren't afraid to take the game to Liverpool. We backed ourselves to cause problems and we led after three minutes, Manu marking his first start in the league by tapping in from close range after good work from Cress on the left.

We'd caught Liverpool by surprise. They didn't know how to react and our dominance was rewarded when I made it 2–0 with a crisp low shot after half an hour. It was special to score in front of the Kop and I celebrated by mimicking Didier Drogba's famous arm-pumping celebration – a tribute to my mate Shorty, who kept doing the same celebration after coming over to my house for a game of football in my garden during the week.

Liverpool could have no complaints. They lost Philippe Coutinho to a red card early in the second half and we didn't panic after I was unfairly sent off for a challenge on James Milner. I didn't touch him – the decision was later overturned – and we coped with being a man down,

Diafra going through in the last 10 minutes to make it 3–0.

It was a performance that made people sit up and really take notice of us. It wasn't a fluke. We were set up well, with me, Cheikhou Kouyaté and Pedro Obiang providing the cover for Dimi and Manu to create, and Slav's positivity gave us so much belief. He sent us out to win every game and he had backing from the board, the additions of Michail Antonio, Nikica Jelavić and Victor Moses before the end of the transfer window bolstering the depth and quality of our squad.

I was optimistic about the team Slav was putting together. There was a different feel at the club, with the frustration that was threatening to spill over by the end of Sam's time in charge no longer an issue, and there was a buzz around Upton Park when we beat Newcastle in our next outing, two cracking goals from Dimi earning us another convincing win.

It had been a while since we'd seen such a positive atmosphere at home. It was a relief to have a connection with the fans again. They were excited about Slav's style of play and they already adored Dimi. They needed to see a player like him in claret and blue. We were strong and powerful under Sam, but we'd never had anyone as talented as Dimi. He shocked me with what he could do with a ball and he wasn't a problem in the dressing room. I'd heard stories about Dimi's behaviour at his previous clubs, but he surprised me with how easily he settled in at West Ham. He was always messing around with the lads and, crucially, his love of a joke at training was matched by his trickery on the pitch.

Nobody could argue with Dimi's impact. Slav loved him, and our run continued when we visited Manchester City. Who cared if we were the underdogs? We weren't scared of anyone – even City. We went on the attack straight away, swept into a 2–0 lead thanks to goals from Sakho and Victor, and held on after Kevin De Bruyne pulled one back for them.

Things were getting silly. I went to the back of the bus after the game and laughed when I saw Cress. Neither of us could believe it. Since when did West Ham start a season by winning at places like Arsenal, City and Liverpool? It was unreal. We were on 12 points after six games, and I was so pleased that the job was going well for Slaven. The significance of leaving Upton Park wasn't lost on anyone. It was on my mind when I woke up every morning. We couldn't ruin the farewell to the Boleyn Ground. We had to go out on a high. We had to keep the run going.

*   *   *

We weren't perfect. We slipped up against a few weaker sides and had to pull off a fair few comebacks from 2–0 down. But we were impeccable against the big boys. They were going through a transitional period and weren't at peak strength, which meant there was an opportunity for an outsider to move in and try to disrupt the established order at the top of the table.

We had as good a chance as anyone of breaking into the top six. Slav had plenty of talent at his disposal, and it wasn't a huge shock when Upton Park witnessed another fantastic win over Chelsea at the end of October. They were a top side, with players like Hazard and Costa up front, but we outplayed them. Zárate put us ahead with a fizzing shot in the first half, Chelsea lost Nemanja Matić to a red card before half-time and we held our nerve after Gary Cahill's equaliser, wearing them down and finding the breakthrough when Andy headed in the winner.

It felt like it was written in the stars. It was fitting that the fans were being treated to so many special moments during our final season at Upton Park. The frustration, though, was that we couldn't push on after beating Chelsea. Injuries slowed our momentum. The big one was losing Dimi for a couple of months after he got hit by a bad challenge during a draw with Everton. Inevitably, we weren't as fluid without our main creative force. The goals dried up, we drew five games in a row and our overcrowded treatment room irritated Slav, who blamed the issue on our training ground, Chadwell Heath. I'd played there for years so it wasn't a problem for me, but Slav argued that it was why we had so many muscle injuries. He was more relaxed when we eventually moved to our new site at Rush Green.

Yet while the injuries were frustrating, forcing us to become more defensive and survive with some dull performances, at least there was an opportunity for squad players to step up. I was intrigued to see whether Michail Antonio would be capable of helping us. He'd found it really challenging after joining us from Nottingham Forest at the end of August. Forest were in the Championship and Mic, whose career began in non-league, needed time to adapt after jumping up to the next level.

The training was far more technical than anything Mic had experienced before and he found the first few months with us painful. He wasn't close to getting in the team and, while he had plenty of strength and speed, it wasn't clear how he was going to fit into Slav's system.

Yet Mic was far from a lost cause. He had a lot of raw ability, and I urged him to stay patient when he told me that he was thinking about going out on loan. 'Mic, everyone knows you can play in the Championship,' I said. 'You've done that, so just stay here and train with good players. And if it doesn't work out for you, then go on loan at the end of the season.'

I'm glad he took my advice on board. Boy did he hit the ground running when Slav finally gave him a chance. His pace and power gave us a new dimension in attack, and he didn't look back after scoring his first goal in claret and blue during a victory over Southampton at the end of December.

It didn't bother Mic that it was one of the weirdest goals ever scored by a West Ham player. He was lying on the pitch when a clearance from a Southampton defender hit him on the head and rebounded into the net, but Mic didn't care how it went in. He was just delighted he'd helped us win a game, and it wasn't long before he'd established himself as a regular starter, his direct running and presence in the box making it impossible for Slav to pick someone else in his place.

Mic's development was incredible. He's one of the most improved players I've ever seen at West Ham. There was so much enthusiasm to his game and the more he played with us, the better he became on the ball. Slowly but surely he smoothed out the rough edges and he became even more dangerous when Slav realised how good Mic was in the air, which we saw when he followed up his goal against Southampton by giving us the lead with a powerful header when Liverpool visited Upton Park four days later.

The Liverpool game was a turning point in our season. Our injury problems were clearing up and our swagger was back. Manu was available again after shaking off a hamstring strain, Andy killed off Liverpool's hopes of a comeback by making it 2–0 with a header in the second half, and there was a huge roar from the crowd when Dimi came off the bench with 25 minutes left.

It was a massive boost to have Dimi back. The sight of him taking out three Liverpool players with an unreal piece of skill as soon as he got on the ball gave us so much inspiration. The shackles were off and the feeling in the dressing room was that we were ready to start causing some damage again.

*   *   *

Champions League qualification was now a genuine possibility. Dimi's return made us believe and we knew that we could score against anyone. We attacked from every angle, threw caution to the wind and didn't worry too much about defending, even though our determination to take as many risks as possible often infuriated our overworked centre-backs.

'That's all right,' Ginge would shout as he watched us flying around at training, 'I'll just f**king mark these five on my own.' Ginge complained about it all the time.

Everyone had permission to bomb on and, despite having a strong defence, we conceded a lot of goals because we attacked so much.

But that was our style. We started games slowly, only to sort ourselves out and win from behind. Our team spirit made us stronger. We were a tightknit group and the dressing room was full of top characters. I got on well with Angelo Ogbonna, who's an amazing guy, and I loved how Cheikhou always came in with a smile on his face.

Players like Cheikhou are so important. He was as honest as they come on the pitch – you could rely on him to run all day, win his tackles and never shy away from challenging for a header – and he was terrific company. If I wasn't feeling good I could always rely on Cheikhou to cheer me up. He always joked around, and I spent a lot of time with him and Sakho, listening to them talk about their upbringing in Senegal.

Those boys were so funny. They had so many stories about life back at home and I always looked forward to Cheikhou calling his dad on FaceTime. I had loads of chats with Cheikhou's dad, who still lived in Senegal, and it wasn't hard to work out why Cheikhou was such a bubbly person.

Cheikhou always made people laugh. I still crack up when I think back to his antics after we fought back from 2–0 down to beat Everton 3–2 at the start of March. We took the train back to London, got on the coach after pulling in at Euston station and were greeted by hundreds of West Ham fans belting out their chant about Dimi, who'd gone and made himself the hero again by scoring the winner in the last minute at Goodison Park.

> We've got Payet, Dimitri Payet!
> I just don't you think you understand!
> He's Super Slav's man, he's better than Zidane!
> We've got Dimitri Payet!

It was the soundtrack to our season – they sang it to the tune of 'Achy Breaky Heart' by Billy Ray Cyrus – but Cheikhou wasn't having it. 'Oh, f**k off,' he went as he ran down to the front of the coach, pulled the door open and held his arms aloft before directing a new chant at the fans.

'We've got Kouyaté! Cheikhou Kouyaté!'

In reality Cheikhou knew it was all about Dimi. By that stage it felt like anything was possible. We were pushing for a place in the top four and it felt like Dimi was going to score every time he stepped up to take a free-kick. He curled one in when we smashed Blackburn 5–1 in the fifth round of the FA Cup, he scored a couple of bangers for France and nobody was fooled whenever Cress ran up to a free-kick, making out he was going to do something more than step over the ball and hand responsibilities over to Dimi.

Cress knew where he was in the pecking order. We called him Decoy Derek and he responded by claiming assists for all the times he stood nearby while Dimi whipped a free-kick into the top corner.

The level was ridiculous. We played Crystal Palace at Upton Park at the start of April and they put seven men in the wall when we won a free-kick on the edge of the area. It still wasn't enough. Initially I thought that Dimi's effort was going over. Instead the ball wobbled through the air before dipping into the top corner, leaving Palace's goalkeeper Wayne Hennessey rooted to the spot and the rest of us trying to work out how Dimi had managed to pull that one off.

Dimi was in the form of his life. His goal put us 2–1 up against Palace and at that stage we appeared to be on course to qualify for the Champions League. Yet Palace made it awkward for us. We lost Cheikhou to a debatable red card and were unable to hold on with 10 men, a 2–2 draw leaving us three points off fourth with seven games to go.

A few bad decisions went against us during that period. We went to Manchester United in the last eight of the FA Cup and were denied a win by the officials failing to spot Bastian Schweinsteiger fouling Darren Randolph when Anthony Martial scored a late equaliser. We drew with

Chelsea and Leicester after having questionable penalties awarded against us in both games.

But there's no point complaining about referees. The truth is we weren't quite good enough. Our philosophy was, 'You score two, we'll score three', but we probably could have done with being a bit tighter at times. We made life difficult for ourselves and it didn't help when Slav had to play Mic out of position at right-back. We'd lost Jenko to a serious knee injury and Sam Byram, who'd made a very promising debut when we drew 2–2 with City in January, kept picking up little niggles. We didn't have anyone else, so Slav was forced to improvise by asking Mic to do a job for the team, even though he didn't really have a defensive bone in his body.

It wasn't the most successful of experiments. We were too open. We should have moved on from our draw with Palace by beating Arsenal, whose defenders were absolutely scared to death of Andy. He loved playing against sides who couldn't handle him physically. His eyes lit up, and no defender could stop him when he was in full swing. You could hear him coming when the ball came into the box and you could see defenders in training thinking, 'Holy shit!' They couldn't do much more than wait for Andy to wipe them out, and we knew that he was capable of destroying any Premier League defence as long as we put the ball in the right areas for him to attack.

It's a shame that injuries stopped him from fulfilling his potential. There was no way of stopping Andy if the service was right, and he was at his best against Arsenal, scoring an inspirational hat-trick that turned a 2–0 deficit into a 3–2 lead.

Again, though, we couldn't get ourselves over the line. We dropped two more vital points after Arsenal pegged us back to 3–3, and there was more disappointment on the way when we played our FA Cup quarter-final replay against United.

It was a weird occasion. We should have won the first game at Old Trafford – Dimi had given us the lead by scoring a free-kick from miles out, only for Martial to force a replay – and the fans thought it was our year. We'd beaten Liverpool at Upton Park in a fourth-round replay, Angelo Ogbonna scoring a last-minute winner in extra-time, and everyone thought we were favourites to beat an inconsistent United side.

But the expectations were too high. The atmosphere was subdued and United, who still had a lot of talent, outplayed us. They deservedly took a 2–0 lead at the start of the second half and my frustration got the better of me when Ander Herrera went down with an injury. I wasn't having it when I saw him wink at the physio. I knew he was trying to waste time, so I decided to pick him up and carry him off the pitch.

I can't explain why I did it. It just felt right at the time and it didn't do us much good in the end. Tonks pulled a goal back for us, but we'd given ourselves too much to do. I was devastated when the final whistle blew. I thought we had a great chance of winning the cup, although the defeat didn't gnaw away at me. Playing in the Premier League was demanding enough from a mental perspective. Losing in the cups hurt, but I never had time to dwell. There was always another game on the way.

*　　*　　*

I knew how to take the rough with the smooth. I played the best football of my career during our first season under Slav and I thought I had a chance of breaking into the England squad for the first time. I was captaining a side challenging for Europe, I was scoring goals from midfield and I don't think that I could have done much more to convince England's manager, Roy Hodgson, to have a closer look at me.

But the call from Hodgson never arrived, I never had a conversation with him about it nor was there any indication from anyone in his backroom staff that I was in his thoughts. Yet my performances were consistently at a high standard and I couldn't help but wonder if I was going to make the standby list for England's squad at Euro 2016 after I scored four goals in victories over Watford and West Brom during the run-in.

It wasn't meant to be. I let go of my dream of playing for England after missing out on that squad. I couldn't understand Hodgson's thinking, but I wasn't bitter. I find it funny when people hound me about never playing for England. Spurs fans love it. One of them had a pop when we got off the coach before one of our games at White Hart Lane.

'Hey, Noble, guess what?'

'What, mate?'

'I've got the same number of England caps as you!'

I had to laugh. That's what football's about. I'd have done the same to a Spurs player if I was in the crowd at West Ham. I don't take myself too seriously. My grandparents on my mum's side are Irish, but I never thought about switching my international allegiance to Ireland. I didn't want to stand in the way of an Irish kid who'd dreamed of representing his country all his life. I only cared about England.

It would have been wonderful to get a cap. Maybe Gareth Southgate, who gives chances to loads of players, would have picked me if he'd been in charge of England when I was at my peak. Yet I've accepted that the timing was never right and I've had a better career than a lot of players who represented England. It was an honour to lead my boyhood club out in the Premier League and I realised how much the fans appreciated me when they packed out Upton Park for my testimonial in March 2016.

I couldn't have wished for a better day. The trains weren't running and there was a storm on the morning of the game, but people still turned up. There wasn't an empty seat in the house and I was delighted that so many West Ham heroes agreed to play. We saw Rio Ferdinand, Paolo Di Canio and Julian Dicks wearing claret and blue shirts again, and I was so happy to have Dean Ashton there. One of the saddest moments I've ever had in football was when Deano was forced to retire in 2009. He wasn't the same after breaking his ankle in 2006. He worked so hard to get back, but we knew it was over when we heard the bone in his ankle clicking when he tried to run during training.

The look on Deano's face was heartbreaking. He was a lovely guy and a superb striker. I marvelled at his finishing in training and I think he would have risen to the very top if he'd stayed fit, but the pain in his ankle was too much. It was agonising to watch a promising career end so soon.

I'm pleased that Deano has accepted his new role in the game. He does loads of punditry work and he seemed to have found some peace when I spoke to him at my testimonial. He even offered the crowd a reminder of his ability, rolling back the years by scoring with a stunning bicycle kick.

I wanted it to be that kind of day. The fans have enough stress watching us on a normal Saturday afternoon. I wanted them to have some fun, drink in the nostalgia and just enjoy a celebration of being West Ham.

It was about being part of a community. I didn't think twice about giving away all the proceeds to three charities close to my heart – Help for Heroes, the DT38 Foundation and Richard House Children's Hospice. I didn't need the money. I cared more about being on the pitch with Sam, Shorty and Robert, my mates from childhood. Those boys have been with me every step of the way. They've stuck by me since we were kids and are more like brothers than mates. They've travelled everywhere to watch me play and I wouldn't have been the person I am today without their support, so I loved it when they saw their shirts hanging off the pegs in the dressing room. That said, I could have done without Robert saving penalties from Chris Cohen and Marlon Harewood. He never misses a chance to mention it. It's no wonder that Chris says that missing that penalty is the biggest regret of his career.

But I cherished those moments. It was special to have lasted so long at West Ham. It was where I'd grown up, where I'd become a man, and England couldn't have been further from my mind when I walked out with my kids by my side before kick-off. I felt blessed when I gazed around that famous old ground. It was the stuff that dreams were made of, the final ever testimonial at Upton Park, and it was going to take something extraordinary to top it.

* * *

There was so much emotion around every home game. The nostalgia grew as our move to the London Stadium edged closer and it seemed that nobody could think about anything other than the big send-off against Manchester United.

Having United as the final visitors to Upton Park made the occasion even bigger. It made it harder to concentrate on our top-four challenge. We were a disaster when we hosted Swansea three days before United came to town. Our minds were elsewhere, nobody wanted to get injured and Swansea caught us off guard, ending our hopes of qualifying for the Champions League by thrashing us 4–1.

Viewed from a distance, it was a waste of a season. We finished seventh after losing 2–1 to Stoke on the final weekend, which was enough to gain entry into the preliminary stages of the Europa League, but we should have been higher. We only missed out on fourth by four points. I don't think we quite realised what a strong position we were in at the time.

Yet it was still a season to savour. The atmosphere at Upton Park was incredible from start to finish and the feeling before playing United was something I'd never experienced before. Even the play-off finals didn't compare. This was different. Usually it took us 15 minutes to reach the ground after boarding the coach at our hotel in Canary Wharf. This time the journey took an hour. The streets were heaving with West Ham fans and I couldn't believe it when I looked out at the sea of claret and blue while the coach was crawling along the Barking Road. There were so many familiar faces in the crowd, and I couldn't have been more pumped up by the time we reached the stadium.

I was desperate for the game to start. The tension grew when kick-off was delayed because the crowd had prevented United from arriving on time. We simply had to wait in the dressing room, and it was a huge relief when we finally went outside to warm up.

It sounds nuts, but nobody was thinking about qualifying for Europe. Nothing mattered more than Upton Park's closing night. I'd never seen anything like it when I walked down the tunnel. The ground was almost full during the warm-up. It was dark, but smoke filled the air and the noise was crackling. 'This is going to be the last ever time I play here,' I thought. I felt emotional. I'd been going to Upton Park since I was a boy. I'd grown up round the corner and inherited the addiction from Dad. Sometimes I'd sneak through the turnstiles with my mates; sometimes I'd simply stood outside with the other kids, waiting for the players to come outside so we could bug them for autographs.

I was lucky. I got Sir Geoff Hurst to sign my school binder. I got shirts from Tomas Repka, who I later played with in the first team, and Sébastien Schemmel, our French right-back. I loved Schemmel. He had an all-action style and his enthusiasm helped him win the Hammer of the Year award in 2002.

Those memories mean so much. It wasn't easy to play at Upton Park when we were losing, but it was an asset when we were playing well. Opposition players loved the atmosphere, but they hated it when the home fans started roaring us on. The intensity was unrivalled, and I loved the family feel. I thought about the people who'd sat next to each other for 30 years. The staff were all West Ham fans. You went to a box and your uncle's mate was working there. You went to the players' lounge and you'd see someone who knew your granddad. That was West Ham's identity. We might not have had the best facilities, but nobody could match the togetherness of our people. It goes further than team spirit. It's a spirit that spreads across every corner of the club, forging lifelong bonds, and I've always tried to make sure nothing breaks that unity.

We're stronger when we're together. Everyone pulled in the same direction when we played against United. The noise was deafening and I could feel the adrenaline pumping through my veins. I was desperate to win and I allowed myself a moment of superstition before kick-off, bending down to kiss the ball when I did the coin toss with Wayne Rooney.

I like to think that kiss helped us on the pitch. Powered on by the crowd, we dominated the first half and took an early lead through Sakho. We were playing with so much belief and I refused to give up hope after United fought back in the second half, going 2–1 up thanks to two break-away goals from Anthony Martial. 'This can't end this way,' I thought. 'This ain't going to end this way. We will score.'

We didn't panic. We trusted in our ability, and I knew we'd score again after Dimi set up Mic for the equaliser with 14 minutes left. I knew United wouldn't hold out when I heard the roar of the crowd. I knew we'd get a chance from a set-play, and, sure enough, we were 3–2 up when Dimi whipped in a free-kick for Winston to head past David de Gea with 10 minutes left.

It was wild. One of my favourite ever pictures of me in a West Ham kit is of me running away and jumping in the air while the fans celebrated behind me. It was such a special moment, and me and Slav both had tears in our eyes at full-time. It was some goodbye. All our families were in the dressing room after the game. Everyone was drinking in the moment, and it was great to see all the legends on the pitch during the post-match parade.

'I don't want this to end,' I thought. 'I don't want to go home.' I stayed in our lounge until 1 a.m., having a beer with a few players and staff members, and despite the celebratory mood I was sad that we were moving on from the place we'd called home for 112 years.

A brave new era was about to begin. A bright future beckoned at the London Stadium. We were growing as a club.

9

Moving Home

It was with a heavy heart that I accepted it was time to leave Upton Park. Unable to expand the ground due to geographical reasons, we were stuck with a capacity of 35,000 and were struggling to find ways to bring in more matchday revenue. From the club's perspective there was no other choice – we needed a bigger stadium if we were going to challenge the top sides. And while some fans had reservations about us moving to Stratford, I was confident that the London Stadium would eventually come to feel like home.

We had to be bold enough to take the next step. I looked at the positives and I was excited at first. The signs were encouraging when we marked our first match in the London Stadium by beating NK Domžale 3–0. The win over the Slovenian minnows took us through to the next round of qualifying for the Europa League and there were more good vibes when we hosted Juventus in a pre-season friendly three days later. The sun was shining, the stadium was rammed and the fans were behind us. 'This is going to be fantastic,' I thought.

Yet I didn't realise how many stumbles there were going to be along the way. A trip to the stadium with Slaven just before the start of the 2016–17 season was an eye-opener. We were surprised to find there was no players' lounge and we both agreed the home dressing room wasn't big enough for us. Changes had to be made. We needed a lounge, and the only way to make more space in the dressing room was to knock through the walls and start again.

Everybody loved the final season at Upton Park, but it now hampered us. Expectations were too high and the owners, who were under pressure to deliver, found themselves fighting an uphill battle to shift the narrative around the bedding-in issues.

The transition was tougher than the board possibly could have imagined. It was a perfect storm. Our signings were disappointing, our performances dipped and we missed out on a place in the Europa League group stage after losing to Astra Giurgiu for the second consecutive year. It didn't take long for some fans to start grumbling. They found it hard to adjust to the change. They didn't like going to a stadium that was still being used for athletics. They weren't happy about the pitch being surrounded by a running track. They said it felt soulless compared with Upton Park, and the atmosphere suffered because the people who liked to sing weren't in the same part of the ground.

It took time to get used to our new surroundings. It was a huge new stadium with more than 60,000 seats and some of the fans weren't used to being as far from the action. There were teething problems, particularly with the green material that covered the running track, which was later changed to claret – something that made a hugely positive difference to the players.

*   *   *

We'd become easy prey. The club was divided, the fans were divided and for a while it was hard to see a way forward. The big dilemma for the board was that we didn't own the ground. We didn't have our own people working there. There was no familiarity with the staff.

It made life unnecessarily challenging. When I turned up at Upton Park it was all, 'Hello, Marky boy, how are you, son?' at the main entrance. But it was colder at the London Stadium. We had to arrive three hours early on a matchday, and I had a baffling exchange with security when I pulled up at the stadium for one of our first games there.

'No, sorry,' the guy said. 'Your number plate's not on the sheet. You can't come in.'

'Sorry, what?'

'Your number plate's not on the sheet,' he replied. 'You can't come in.'

'Mate, I've got to play in three hours,' I said. 'You've got to let me in.'

'Sorry, you'll have to ring the player liaison officer.'

I was raging. I'd have driven straight through if a huge electrical barrier wasn't blocking my way. I could feel my blood pressure rising. A team-mate drove up behind me and I had to explain why I was holding up the queue. It was unbelievable.

But it didn't just happen to me. The staff didn't know who we were. On another occasion I watched security stop Cress from walking down the tunnel. 'No, mate,' the guy said. 'Excuse me, you haven't got a pass. You can't come down here.'

The situation was made even more absurd by the fact the tunnel was decorated by a huge canvas of the team. 'Mate, have a look behind you,' Cress said. 'There's a f**king four-metre picture of me – obviously I can come down here!'

It was an infuriating situation. Our families had trouble as well. They wouldn't be let in to our lounge to see us and there were times when Carly was told her name wasn't on the list when she turned up at the stadium.

'Carly Noble.'

'You're not down to come in.'

'But my husband's playing in 15 minutes!'

It was a mission for Carly to get through. My phone would be switched off in my locker, so there was no way of reaching me, and I wouldn't find out until after the game. Then all hell would break loose. I'd be shouting and screaming at everyone.

'How the f**k can this be allowed to happen?!'

Yet it was a while before anything changed. We built relationships at the stadium. I told them: 'The people there now don't know who the players are. And you need them around the dressing room as well. We've got to be there three hours before the game, and we go and chill out in the lounge. But we're not allowed to go anywhere.' Luckily, they listened to what we were saying – things improved and I've got a great relationship with the staff at the stadium now.

I'd been at the club since I was 11 and a geezer who didn't support West Ham was stopping me at the gate because my name wasn't on his clipboard. It was tough to take. The organisation should have been better.

Yet it would have been easier if we'd been playing well. The fans would have been more patient. As it was, we were a mess on and off the pitch. Football's a game of confidence. We looked fine when we hosted Watford at the start of September. We played some great stuff and took a 2–0 lead when Dimi set up Mic with a rabona cross midway through the first half.

It was like the All-Stars at one stage. But one mistake from Adrián changed everything. Somehow Watford fought back to make it 2–2 before half-time. We went to pieces at the back and unravelled in the second half, offering little resistance as Watford took control and won 4–2.

It all went wrong after that game. I was in agony after the Watford midfielder Étienne Capoue accidentally stood on my hand and put a stud through the soft part at the base of my thumb. The wound needed to be closed, and I was in even more pain when the doctor managed to put a stitch in my nerve.

'This can't be normal,' I said, but the doctor said the cut would open up again if they took the stitches out. The solution was for me to wear a wrist brace when we visited West Brom a week after our defeat to Watford. We were 3–0 down at half-time and I couldn't continue.

'I shouldn't be in this much pain,' I said. 'Every time I move, I'm getting shooting pains down my fingers. You've got to take these stitches out.'

It was a repeat of our 4–0 defeat to West Brom under Big Sam. Back then it was my stomach playing up; this time it was my thumb. 'Why have you done this to yourself again?' I thought. 'Why can't you just say you can't play.'

I hadn't realised how much we use our hands during a game. You need to push opponents and hold them off, but I couldn't do anything. It was such a relief when the doctor finally took the stitches out after the game.

Yet the improvement in my physical condition wasn't a minor consolation. We ended up losing 4–2 to West Brom and I snapped when we lost 3–0 at home to Southampton a week later. I didn't hold back when I was interviewed on live TV after the game. Fans might be fickle, but they aren't stupid. They know when things aren't right and I didn't want to pretend that everything was OK. I was as frustrated as anyone, and I was never frightened to tell the truth. 'It could have been six,' I said. 'On the bright side I don't think it can get any worse.'

* * *

We were in a bad place again. We had nobody capable of stepping up in attack after Andy and Diafra picked up long-term injuries. The boys who came in during the summer were walking into such a tough situation. I didn't blame the likes of Jonathan Calleri, Gökhan Töre, Sofiane Feghouli and Simone Zaza for struggling. None of them had any experience of English football, and it's been shown time and time again that there's nothing harder than for a foreign player to impress when they join a side who are in terrible form.

It was the wrong way for us to go. Zaza had done well in Serie A and was an Italy international, but he wasn't suited to the Premier League. Ashley Fletcher, who joined on a free transfer from United, was just a kid. André Ayew, signed for £20m from Swansea City, was hit and miss on the right wing. It wasn't a surprise when the goals dried up.

I could tell that Slav was frustrated. We were blunt in the final third and we'd forgotten how to defend. Shoddy recruitment cost us. Slav was forced to try so many players at right-back. He experimented with Mic, but he wanted to play in attack. He asked Håvard Nordtveit to fill in, but he was a midfielder. He persisted with Sam Byram, but he couldn't stay fit. It wasn't acceptable. We never had a balanced back four and opponents didn't take long to work out where to hurt us.

It was an avoidable situation. It was a shame we allowed Tonks to join Crystal Palace that summer, even though he'd become fed up with Slav playing him as a right-back. We missed him so much. He was a top defender, better than a lot of people realised, and he was great around the dressing room.

I loved Tonks – although admittedly I did argue with him all the time. I went head to head with Tonks when we beat Everton in the FA Cup in January 2015 and I never turned down a chance to wind him up.

There was the time me, Matty Upson and a few of the boys covered the windscreen on Tonks's new BMW X5 with Vaseline. Getting that stuff off is nigh on impossible. Tonks was livid. I saw him outside with a bucket, trying to clean up the mess, and he didn't take it well when I laughed at him. He booted the bucket in the air, marched off to one of the pitches and sat on his own for an hour because he was so angry.

I always knew how to get under Tonks's skin. We had another row just before going away on a golfing trip together. We had training before our flight and it all kicked off when Tonks complained about my team getting all the decisions during a five-a-side game. 'Oh, f**king Nobes is the captain, yeah?' he raged. 'You're f**king giving him everything.'

Before I knew it we had each other by the throat. Tonks was foaming at the mouth and I continued to needle him after we got pulled apart. 'Tonks, you still coming to golf?' I said. 'You don't have to if you don't want to.'

'F**k off, Nobes, you f**king prick.'

But it was all forgotten when we were back in the changing room. We went on the trip and had a fantastic time. Yet I still can't resist a chance to have a little nibble. Tonks used to live 10 doors down from me and I came up with a way to prank him just after he joined Palace. I'd just bought a new Mavic Pro drone and was testing it out with Lenny in the garden when I had a thought. 'Len,' I said, 'let's fly down to Tonks's house.'

It was hilarious. I was watching Tonks on my phone and I assumed he'd know it was me. But he went mad. He was shushing it away and swearing at it. He even ran over to his barbecue, picked up some lumps of coal and started throwing them at the drone. He looked so angry in his Palace tracksuit. Me and Lenny were crying with laughter, and I was still talking about it when I went to training the next day.

'Boys, you should have seen Tonks last night,' I said to Andy and Cress. 'He was trying to smash my drone up with charcoals out of his barbecue.'

The only problem was I hadn't told Tonks it was me. Andy bumped into him in London a few days later and let the cat out of the bag. Tonks was fuming when Andy asked about the drone. 'What?' he said. 'That was f**king Nobes?'

I got a text from Tonks later that evening, claiming he was going to blow the drone up. I didn't mind, Tonks always made me laugh. He used to lose his head all the time, but we never had a proper falling out and I always backed him to perform on the pitch.

We didn't replace Tonks properly. There was a big hole at right-back, but signing Álvaro Arbeloa didn't solve anything. Although Arbeloa had won loads at Real Madrid, he wasn't able to show his quality for us. He was a fitness freak, a top professional and a nice guy, but he struggled with injuries and his frustration got the better of him when he elbowed a speedy young winger during a reserve match. Slav wasn't impressed. He pulled us all inside and reprimanded Arbeloa, who responded by having a go back at Slav.

There was no coming back from that. Arbeloa didn't hang around when Slav told him to go back to Spain. Two hours later Arbeloa sent a photo of himself to our group chat. He was already on the plane home. It summed things up.

*   *   *

The prospect of going down was a constant concern. Relegation would have been a catastrophe for the club. The sense that everything was falling apart grew when Dimi told Slav that he wanted to leave at the start of January.

The news left everyone reeling. Dimi was our star and there was no sign of any trouble during the first half of the season. He came off the bench to rescue us with a trademark free-kick when we were struggling to see off Accrington Stanley in the League Cup, he scored an incredible solo goal to earn us a point against Middlesbrough and there didn't appear to be anything wrong when he helped us draw 2–2 with Liverpool at the start of December.

I was upset when Slav announced that Dimi had handed in a transfer request. Dimi made my life as West Ham captain so beautiful for 18 months. When you have something like that, you don't want to see it go. You want to hold on to it for ever.

Yet Dimi, who was quite an emotional person, had made up his mind. He wasn't afraid to air his feelings and he made it clear that he wanted to go back to Marseille. I think he was dealing with some issues at home and I would have helped him if I'd known what was going on behind the scenes. I wish he'd opened up to me. Family comes before football, and I'd have gone to the owners on Dimi's behalf if he'd asked me for help.

The situation could have been handled with more care. The fans have forgiven Dimi now and he sent me a lovely video message when I retired, but it was hard when he left. The gloom deepened. People said we were mad to leave Upton Park. We were supposed to be moving to the next level, but our best player was gone and we were in danger of being sucked into the bottom three.

Fortunately we still had enough quality. Yet I was struggling. I wasn't moving properly. We lost at home to Chelsea at the start of March and I was at fault for their first goal. I dithered in possession when I should have crossed the ball, N'Golo Kanté tackled me and Hazard scored on the counterattack. At the time it seemed like I was messing around. Looking back, the reality was I was nowhere near 100 per cent fit.

Once again I was putting my body on the line. We scrapped our way to a few decent results and had a chance to secure our survival when we hosted Spurs with three games left.

However, I'd started to experience really bad pain in my stomach two weeks before the Spurs game. I went to see a specialist, who identified the problem. 'You've got two hernias next to your belly button,' he said. 'That's what's causing your pain.'

I was in serious discomfort. I went to Slav to tell him I needed an operation, but he pleaded with me to wait. 'Mark, just play against Spurs,' he said. 'If we win you can have the op.'

Although I'd promised myself I wouldn't risk my health again after what I'd gone through against West Brom, I couldn't say no to Slav. I dosed myself up on tablets, played through the pain and helped us hold on after Manu gave us a 1–0 lead in the second half.

I really didn't feel like celebrating. We were safe but my stomach was killing me. I went to training the next day and this time I didn't listen when Slav asked me to delay the surgery until we'd played Liverpool in our final home game. 'Boss, I'm in f**king agony,' I said. 'I need to have this operation. It's worrying me.'

Slav couldn't argue. I went to hospital and they told me I'd be out for an hour and 20 minutes. Little did they realise they'd find six hernias when they opened me up. Or that my abs had split in the middle. It was all through wear and tear. I'd given so much to West Ham and this was the price I had to pay. It wasn't a simple procedure any more. The doctors had to perform keyhole surgery, repair the hernias, stitch my abs together and then insert a big mesh to hold everything together.

Obviously it took longer than 80 minutes. I was out for six hours and was dosed up on all sorts when I woke up. It wasn't fun and I could have done without a nurse coming in to stick a big tablet up my arse.

Then there was Carly. She thought the operation wasn't going to take long and she was a nervous wreck when it went on for six hours. She didn't eat anything and was in a state when I woke up.

'How are you feeling, babe?' she said.

'I feel lovely,' I said, letting the painkillers do the talking.

'I'm going to have to leave you,' she said. 'I'm starving.'

That was an understatement. Carly fainted as soon as she tried to stand up. Now it was my turn to feel pain. Carly had passed out on top of me because the hunger had made her so light-headed, and there was no way I could lift her up. I couldn't use my abs; the best I could do was fling her over so I could press the emergency button to call the nurse for help.

Thankfully Carly was only out for about 10 seconds. She was fine after they gave her some food, whereas I had a tough recovery in front of me. I was out for the rest of the season and I couldn't even move when I coughed. I was no use to anyone and my mood didn't improve when I watched us lose 4–0 to Liverpool on TV.

It was another poor performance and Slav was hurting when he called me after the game.

'Nobes, how are you?' he said.

'Boss, I'm in so much pain.'

'F**k,' Slav said. 'Well, let me assure you of something; you're not in as much pain as I'm f**king in at the minute.'

*　　*　　*

It was a demoralising time for everyone. We were relieved to have stayed up, and at least we had a chance to regroup before the next season. I recovered from my surgery in time for pre-season, and there was renewed optimism when we brought in Joe Hart, Pablo Zabaleta, Javier Hernández and Marko Arnautović during the summer.

But the positivity didn't last long. There weren't many happy faces when we went on a pre-season tour to Germany. The hotel that Slav chose had definitely gone downhill since he'd stayed there with the Croatia national team. We were stuck in the middle of nowhere for two weeks, unable to have proper conversations with our families because of the terrible Wi-Fi, and after a few days we felt our only option was to tell Slav that we wanted to go home.

Yet Slav was too honourable to go back on the promises he'd made to our opponents. He knew that playing us was a big deal for them, so he decided that we were going to see it out until the end.

I think that Slav's hope was that we'd give ourselves a chance of turning the corner if we trained well on that trip. Yet it was a miserable experience. We had to do our gym work in our training centre and we were astonished to find that the goals weren't lined up with each other correctly when we turned up for one of the friendlies.

It was hardly the best way to prepare and, sure enough, we made an awful start to the 2017–18 season. We were bottom of the league after losing our first three games and Slav, who always wore his heart on his sleeve, wasn't happy when he missed out on a few of his targets at the end of the transfer window.

The pressure affected him. He was frustrated with the situation, he couldn't get the players he wanted and he found it impossible to ignore the constant speculation over his future in the media. 'Once the box is open, the press just don't let it close,' he told me. 'They're relentless.'

It's so difficult for a manager when they're not doing well. It's rare to see them recover, particularly when it starts to feel like the next bad result will lead to the sack, and Slav knew that time was running out. In the end I think he was relieved when the board decided to make a change. Slav had a lot of belief in his players and his staff (his former assistant, Edin Terzić, has gone on to manage Borussia Dortmund), and he backed himself to set up a team the right way. After a while, though, his methods stopped working. The transition to the new ground disrupted us, the recruitment was mixed and as players we had to take responsibility for our failure to perform at a high enough standard.

It was an accumulation of little setbacks, gradually building until it became overwhelming. There was a lot of talk about our low running stats towards the end of Slav's time, but it's easy to point to a lack of fitness when a team's form is rubbish. In reality the training hadn't changed from Slav's first season in charge. The fitness stats were the same. I don't think there was anything wrong with Slav's conditioning work.

All the same it was clear that something had to change when Liverpool thrashed us 4–1 at the London Stadium at the start of November. We were all over the place, and the toxic atmosphere was summed up by the moment when I picked up possession in our half and realised that none of my team-mates wanted to show for the ball, only for the fans to boo me when I turned and played a pass back to Joe Hart.

It was horrendous. Slav took me off and I sat there fuming for the rest of the game. 'F**k me,' I thought. 'I've given my life to this club for 15 years and I'm getting booed.'

But that's just the way it goes sometimes. The game was live on BT Sports and Steven Gerrard, who was in the studio as a pundit, sent me a message later that evening. 'Look, Nobes, I've been through that myself where it's not going right and you're the captain and every-one expects it from you,' he wrote. 'You can't actually do it on your own, but you've just got to lace your boots up and go again.'

Stevie's advice made me realise that I had to lead by example. I was gutted when Slav's departure was confirmed, but I was ready to dig in after being told that David Moyes was replacing him. It was what the club needed.

I didn't care that people had written David off after his spells at Manchester United, Real Sociedad and Sunderland. He had a point to prove to the world. David was still a top manager and I was impressed when I spoke to him for the first time. It was clear that he wasn't going to take any nonsense and he was blunt when he introduced himself to the squad. 'Look,' he said. 'You don't run, you don't play.'

There was no negotiating. David's first game was a disappointment, a 2–0 defeat away to Watford, but he backed himself. He wasn't worried about the fans not wanting him and he didn't flinch after we lost 4–0 to Everton at the end of November.

Loads of people were tipping us to go down at that stage. Luckily the dressing room wasn't broken, and while we picked up one point from the new manager's first four games, I could see that we were slowly improving. David made us more solid by changing our formation to a back five. It transformed some players. Arthur Masuaku thrived at left wing-back and our attempts to shift to a counter-attacking style were helped by Marko Arnautović building a little connection with Manu up front.

Marko was a different player under David. He'd been underwhelming under Slav and needed someone to give him a jolt. We all knew the talent was there. Marko was some player and he was one hell of a character. I knew he was an emotional guy after playing against him when he was at Stoke. Me and Kev Nolan spent one game giving it to him for 90 minutes, and I didn't hold back when Marko tumbled to the floor. I pulled his hair and told him to get up, at which point he jumped to his feet and towered over me while we continued to exchange words.

Obviously that was all forgotten when he joined West Ham. We had a laugh about it and I was expecting big things from him. Yet it didn't happen for him to begin with. He got sent off in one of his first games and was ineffective when we played him on the left wing.

Perhaps he needed a bit of confrontation. He responded when David got stuck into him. David was on him all the time, ordering him to run for the team, and the tough love had the desired effect. Suddenly we saw the real Marko Arnautović. I loved having him up front. He was prepared to run in behind and I knew he'd always be available for a ball over the top. It made us a much more effective team.

* * *

We were far more threatening in the final third after Marko perked up. He scored the only goal when David picked up his first win in our 1–0 defeat of Chelsea at the London Stadium at the start of December. His pace, power and skill caused so many problems, and we appeared to be moving away from trouble after Marko provided more inspiration during big away wins over Huddersfield and Stoke.

Yet the fans still weren't convinced. They were still not used to the stadium, and we came under fire after the January transfer window ended with us buying Jordan Hugill from Preston, loaning João Mário from Internazionale and bringing in an ageing Patrice Evra on a free transfer.

Our form dipped after January. The anger became impossible to contain. An explosion was inevitable. A lot of fans weren't happy with the club and they even started arguing among themselves over plans to stage a protest outside the ground before we played Burnley at home on 10 March.

The situation had reached boiling point. I'm West Ham, so I knew about the problems within the fanbase. Nothing escapes my attention. People showed me the rows that were taking place on social media, although my main concern was looking after the club and my team-mates. I was in a tricky situation. My mates were on at me all the time, but I'm a loyal person. I had a good relationship with

David Sullivan and David Gold. They were always ready to step up when I asked for help.

Equally, I understood why the fans were riled up. It's hard when something you love so much falls on hard times. The move wasn't going to plan and everything went wrong when we played Burnley. We missed loads of chances in the first half and it all kicked off when we went 1–0 down in the 66th minute.

I couldn't believe it when a fan ran onto the pitch. I saw the guy heading in the direction of the chairmen, and although I knew he wouldn't be able to get to them I felt that I had to step in. I don't mind if fans demonstrate outside or from their seats, but invading the pitch is never the right way to make your voice heard. I wasn't having it and I didn't think twice about tackling the protester to the ground before he could get any further.

It was my way of saying, 'Look, I'm a f**king West Ham fan. I've supported the team since I was born. But you don't run on the field of play.'

I was as frustrated as anyone. I trained hard every day and it hurt when we lost. Yet it's not fair to affect the games and disturb the players. It made me see red. I completely lost my head and I was lucky that Joe Hart, who's a big, strong guy, ran over to pull me away.

I was fuming. I saw our security guys on the touchline and tore into them, even though I love them to bits and knew it wasn't really their fault. I wasn't particularly repentant when the referee, Lee Mason, came over to have a word.

'Mark, I can't let it go,' he said. 'I'm going to have to do something about this.'

'Mate, are you f**king sure or what?' I said. 'After what's gone on here? Do me a favour.'

To be fair to Lee, he kept his cards in his pocket. Sending me off wouldn't have helped the situation. I was deeply saddened by the sight of hundreds of fans gathering below the directors' box to take aim at the owners. I didn't feel proud to play for West Ham. I was embarrassed. This was the club I'd supported all my life and I knew we were going to be a mockery in the press for the next couple of weeks.

I hated every minute of it. I hated losing 3–0 to Burnley and I hated how the protest got out of hand. I wasn't overly bothered when the fan who got on to the pitch contacted me to apologise. He'd made his decision, and I stood by mine to intervene. I felt it was my job to protect West Ham's image and make sure that nothing happened to my team-mates.

Yet I'd put too much responsibility on my shoulders. I was utterly devastated and I couldn't hold it in when I got home. I tried to relax by watching some TV, but the dam burst when Carly came over to give me a cup of tea. I couldn't stop the tears from rolling down my cheeks.

'I can't believe what's gone on today,' I said. 'I never thought I'd witness something like that as a West Ham fan.'

Carly understood what I was going through. She'd seen me fight tooth and nail for West Ham since I was a boy – but she also knew that I couldn't do it on my own. 'It isn't just on you,' she said. 'It's not all your fault. There are other players in the team.'

Carly was right. Something that really gave me strength was how the manager responded in the dressing room after the game. We were due to fly to Miami the following morning and he was adamant that we weren't going to stay at home. 'I don't give a f**k what's happened today,' he said. 'We're still going away. I don't care what shit you get from the press. We're going away as a team. We'll spend some time together and we're going to come back a better team for it.'

*   *   *

It was brilliant leadership from David. A lot of managers would have worried about the backlash and bottled it. He couldn't care less. David's priority was the team. He was the boss and it showed us that he was on our side. 'Thank f**k someone else around here has got a set of bollocks,' I thought.

We needed to see that strength from our manager. We were also grateful that the owners paid for the flights and put us up in a five-star hotel. It was a way of showing that we were valued. Some fans don't like us heading off on these trips because they think the players are just on a jolly, but I think they're invaluable. Going away is great for morale. It's a chance to learn more about your team-mates. You have a drink together, but then you go and knock on each other's door at 5.30 a.m. to make sure nobody misses the bus to training. It makes you tighter as a team, and going to Miami gave us a chance to escape all the noise back home.

We had to stick together. I agreed with Andy, who wasn't fit at the time, when he told me it wasn't right that the injured players weren't going to come. I went straight to the manager. 'Boss, this ain't just about 15 or 16 players,' I said. 'This is about the whole squad, and the injured players should come with us. We're going to need them when they're fit in a month's time.'

Luckily the gaffer saw my point of view. Nobody was left behind. Andy came along and helped out the coaching staff, and I knew he was still going to have a say on our season. Sure enough, it was Andy who came up with the goods when we needed someone to earn us a vital point when we were losing 1–0 to Stoke during the run-in.

Fortunately the storm clouds had starting to drift away by that stage. Our trip to Miami worked wonders and we were a different side on our return to England. The pressure was immense when we hosted Southampton at the end of March, but we destroyed them. João Mário scored a great goal from the edge of the area and we were 3–0 up at half-time after Marko met a cross from Arthur with an incredible volley.

I was delighted to see the team embracing the challenge. There were a lot of big characters in our dressing room – people like Harty, Angelo, Winston, Ginge, Cress and Javier Hernández – and we were also helped by the emergence of a kid who's gone on to become one of the best midfielders in the Premier League.

I'd first seen Declan Rice up close during our disastrous pre-season tour of Germany. I was blown away when I saw him train. He was playing as a centre-back at the time, and the one thing that stuck in my mind was when he intercepted a pass, stepped out from the back and hit a diagonal ball out to the left wing with a lovely bit of fade on it. 'That was f**king good,' I thought as I turned to look at Dec. 'That was really good.'

It looked like it came so naturally to him. I realised we had a proper player on our hands and I took it upon myself to look after Dec. He didn't talk much, but he was a great kid and he loved it when we bantered him. It already felt like he belonged. While I made sure to teach him do the right things at the right time, I knew he was destined for the top. I'd already come to terms with the fact that he'd eventually keep me out of the team and take the armband off me. 'This ain't going to be a short-term thing,' I thought. 'He's going to go on and play hundreds of games.'

Dec was so confident. He didn't shrink when, during one of his first appearances as a professional, he gave away the opening goal during a 3–0 defeat to Newcastle and got taken off at half-time by Slav. It would have hurt most players, but not Dec. His ability was matched by his self-belief. Being singled out by the manager didn't affect him.

It's why I knew he'd cope when David publicly criticised him for gifting Arsenal a goal when they beat us 4–1 in April 2018. The manager's not stupid. He knew he had a top player on his hands, but he wanted to make sure that Dec learnt from his mistakes. The Premier League is unforgiving. There's no hiding place and David was never afraid to dig a player out. He's the best I've seen at getting a message across in the dressing room. He'd hammer you to your face and tell you like it is if you weren't doing your job, but it would never be personal. It was always for the good of the team and it was impossible not to respect his man-management.

West Ham needed that honesty. David was a breath of fresh air and, having taken over when we were in a horrible position, he managed to keep us up with something to spare. We were almost home and dry after winning 2–0 at Leicester with three games left. João Mário scored the opener and I made the points safe when I smashed a volley past Ben Hamer from 25 yards early in the second half.

I knew I had to hit it when a clearance came my way. I remembered Teddy Sheringham asking me what went through my mind when I scored my first West Ham goal in 2007. This time I thought about everything. The ball was at a good height and it all went in slow motion. 'Right,' I thought. 'Hit this down into the ground, sort of low, with a bit of cut across it so it fades.'

It was perfection. I didn't even feel the ball hit my foot before it swerved into the bottom corner, I'd caught it so well. It was such an important moment, and the points were ours. The journey home was class. We knew we were finally safe when Southampton drew at Everton in the late kick-off. It was time to celebrate. The manager put the music on, everyone on the bus was dancing and I felt emotional when I got a message from Tara Warren, one of the directors at the club. It was a link to a Frank Sinatra song, 'It Had to Be You'. It was Tara's way of saying, 'You fought on the pitch with our fans and now you've scored the goal to keep us up.'

She was right. It had been one hell of a roller-coaster. It was a relief to be able to relax when we hosted Manchester United next. They only needed a point to secure second place and it was plain to see that José Mourinho, who was United's manager at the time, knew how much of an achievement that would be with his squad. 'Nobes, come on,' José said when I saw him in the referee's office before the game. 'I just need a point for second. I'll take you out for lunch if we get a point.'

José had set his stall out. United played defensively and settled for a 0–0 draw. Yet they didn't look like a happy team, and I think that Paul Pogba, their enigmatic French midfielder, let out some of his frustration when he clashed with me towards the end of the game.

I could tell that Paul didn't like how United were playing. It was obvious from his facial expression, and when I nicked the ball off him he responded with a tackle that caught a nerve on the side of my knee. I saw red, swung round to confront him and ended up sticking my finger up his nose when I grabbed his face, which was met by him giving some back to me and swinging me round.

I can laugh about it now. We got pulled apart and when I left our dressing room after the game I saw Lenny standing there with his arm around Paul. 'F**king hell, Len!' I said. 'You're f**king loyal, ain't ya?'

It was water under the bridge. I had a chat with Paul and forgot about it. I understood his frustration. United are such a great club. I love what they stand for – they're my second team and I had so many memorable moments against them – but it's been a struggle for them since Sir Alex Ferguson retired. No manager's quite been able to succeed at Old Trafford and it's difficult for the players who join United because the expectations are so high.

But at least our manager was finally moving on from his time at United. We were starting to find our feet under David Moyes and I really enjoyed myself when we beat Everton 3–1 in our final game. It was the perfect end to a difficult season and I went away thinking that we were back on track. It didn't feel like anything had to change.

10

Turning the Corner

I got on well with David Moyes. He'd saved us from relegation and I wanted him to continue in the job. Yet it wasn't to be. The board had only given David a six-month contract and they were reluctant to reward with him a longer deal after the season ended.

The fans thought that we needed a bigger name and, given the season we'd had, I understand why a crowd-pleasing appointment was made. Manuel Pellegrini had worked for Real Madrid and won the league with Manchester City, and the board were prepared to back him given his record.

Manuel was given the licence to do as he pleased after he was appointed. I thought he was going to be in charge for a long time. He got to work quickly, asking the board to make Mario Husillos our new director of football. Manuel was totally set in his ways. Like all the top managers he had this inner belief that his style of football would bring us success. He never deviated from his philosophy. He trusted his players and, while we didn't do a lot of work on team play and shape, I was confident that he was going to make us better.

I had a lot of time for Manuel and his staff. The manager's deadpan style made him slightly mysterious, and I realised that it was impossible to tell whether or not he was joking when he congratulated me after we beat Wycombe Wanderers during pre-season. 'You played good today,' he said. 'If you want tomorrow off, you have tomorrow off. You're the captain.'

I was completely taken aback. 'Surely I can't have a day off in pre-season,' I thought, but Manuel had walked off before I'd a chance to ask if he was being serious. I didn't know what I was meant to do, so I had to ring the physio to find out if I'd really been singled out for special treatment.

'No,' he said. 'We're all in.'

Manuel was having me on. He liked to test his players, with his record suggesting that his man-management style was going to work. He was fondly remembered by a lot of his players and he was convinced that he'd be able to repeat what he'd achieved at Malaga and Villarreal, both of whom he'd lifted out of mid-table obscurity in Spain and transformed into Champions League contenders.

In that context we looked like a good fit for him and, crucially, he was given access to the kind of funds that weren't available at the club prior to the stadium move and, at the time, to his predecessors at West Ham. We strengthened our attack by breaking our transfer record with the signing of Felipe Anderson from Lazio. We bought Andriy Yarmolenko from Borussia Dortmund and brought Łukasz Fabiański in to be our new No1. Jack Wilshere and Ryan Fredericks came in on free transfers, Issa Diop and Fabián Balbuena provided more competition in central defence, and Lucas Pérez and Carlos Sánchez boosted our squad depth.

It was a whirlwind. Manuel made a lot of changes and I simply hoped that the signings were going to work out. Although the spending heightened expectations, we were still a work in progress, so we were handed a chance to test ourselves when we visited Liverpool on the opening day of the season.

Manuel didn't want to adjust his system. We went to Anfield to win. We played an attacking line-up, and there was a lot of excitement about Dec moving out of defence and starting in midfield. I didn't detect any nerves from the kid when I asked him how he was feeling before the game.

'Yeah,' he said. 'It's just another game. I can't wait.'

'Man, he isn't going to have to worry about anything with that attitude,' I thought – other, that is, than the quality of Liverpool's midfield. Me and Jack accompanied Dec in a midfield three, but Liverpool simply ran through us. We simply weren't ready. Manuel wanted to play a high defensive line, but we weren't used to it yet and could have no complaints about Liverpool thrashing us 4–0.

I think that Manuel tried to move too quickly. Even though I admired his vision, we just weren't good enough to implement it and he put himself under too much pressure, especially as his signings didn't hit the ground running.

The situation didn't improve after our trip to Anfield. We took nothing from our next two games, losing to Bournemouth and Arsenal, and I snapped after a last-minute defeat to Wolves left us rooted to the bottom of the table.

The performance wasn't acceptable. We were pointless after our first four games – just as we were when we got relegated in 2011 – and I was already in a bad mood after being left on the bench. It was time to rattle a few cages when we trooped back into the dressing room after losing to Wolves.

'You lot f**king all think you're superstars,' I said. 'You're not. You're at West Ham for a reason. If you're superstars you wouldn't be here. The fans expect you to work hard, run and chase. It's not f**king Disneyland. You need to f**king buck your ideas up.'

I didn't hold back. The new boys had to adjust to the Premier League and I didn't think we were playing at a high enough intensity. I had to deliver a few home truths and before I knew it I was squaring up to Marko, who'd been with us now for just over a year. I always like to have a go at the big ones. I knew Marko would have a go back, although I did wonder if I'd made a mistake when he stood up and moved towards me. He looked like a bear, and I knew I'd be in trouble if he got hold of me.

Yet it was time for some honesty. I wanted to give the new boys a shock and Marko soon settled down, though I was still angry when a few of the lads sat next to me. I looked at Cress, who had a knowing smile on his face.

'You shat yourself there,' he said. 'As soon as Marko got up you f**king started pedalling backwards.'

Suddenly it was open season on me. The lads spent the next few days taking the piss about me running away from Marko. It seemed I'd done for my bit for team spirit.

*   *   *

I didn't ever hold a grudge against anyone. I was good mates with Marko when we came into training. He's a great guy – caring, loud and funny. He drives mad cars and has an outgoing personality, and I never had a problem with him. His ability was incredible. I know he played for some top sides, but he should have been one of the best. He was capable of beating sides on his own and he was out of this world when we moved on from our defeat to Wolves by winning 3–1 at Everton.

It was the first time we looked like Manuel's team. We had a good bond and a lot of talented players. Felipe was an incredible athlete – quick, strong and committed. He didn't always look like he was trying hard, but his stats were really good and his form was phenomenal during his first six months with us.

With Felipe flying, we began to play some good football. Pablo Zabaleta was still going strong at right-back. I had so much respect for Zaba. He'd won loads of trophies at City, but he didn't come to West Ham just to lie around. He still did all the right things in training and his experience was a massive help in the dressing room.

Yet we couldn't quite hit a consistent run of form. We would have been better if our decision to sign Jack had paid off. Manuel was convinced that he could help Jack rediscover his form and I was excited when he joined. He was a beautiful footballer. I always found Jack a tough opponent when we played Arsenal, and I thought he was going to become one of the best midfielders in the world when I watched him shine against Pep Guardiola's great Barcelona side in 2011.

If only Jack had enjoyed more luck. His greatest strength was that he would dribble with the ball and release it at the very last second, just as you tried to tackle him. Yet injuries had robbed Jack of that crucial burst of speed. He couldn't build any momentum and he found it hard to keep up with Manuel's training.

But Jack was still a great person to have around the place. I have a lot in common with him and we quickly became friends. Characters like Jack lift the mood when you're struggling. He loved getting involved with the banter. Jack didn't blink when we glued his trainers to the floor after he signed. He wasn't short of imagination. One of his best pranks was putting a whole tub of protein powder in Cress's locker, balancing it so it fell out as soon as the door was opened.

Poor Cress. He's a worrier, but Jack didn't care. He nicked Cress's room key when we were away during pre-season. He crept upstairs, lifted the sheets off his bed and covered the mattress in protein powder before putting everything back in its place.

Cress didn't suspect a thing. He came out the shower, nice and clean, and immediately jumped on his bed. The powder went everywhere, covering Cress from head to toe.

At least the abuse went in both directions. Jack went too far when he pissed in a bucket and put it against the door of Snods's hotel room. It wet everything when the door was opened, but Snods wasn't having it. He went up to Jack's room, took a shit on the bathroom floor and called down to reception to say that he'd had an accident.

Jack didn't have a clue when housekeeping turned up and asked if he needed help. 'What are you talking about?' he said, only to realise what had happened when he went into the bathroom.

The dressing room was carnage back then. Players miss that camaraderie when they retire. We know we wouldn't get away with it in a normal workplace, but footballers live by their own rules. We were constantly trying to catch each other out and our spirit kept us together during difficult times.

We still trained hard. We were solid at home, beating Arsenal and Manchester United and drawing with Chelsea and Liverpool. The only flashpoint came when Marko pushed for a move in January after receiving a massive offer from a club in the Chinese Super League. The fans were furious with him, but I didn't hold it against Marko. Football's a short career and, unlike me, he had no prior affiliation with West Ham. He loved the club and the fans, but he had every right to try to earn as much as possible.

I never stood in the way of anyone who wanted to leave for more money or for family reasons, so it didn't affect my relationship with Marko. The only disappointment was that we were losing our best striker. While we managed to keep him in January by giving him a new deal, his desire to move to China never went away and he eventually got his wish when he handed in another transfer request after we finished Manuel's first season in tenth place.

It was a big blow. We'd already made changes to how we defended, and losing Marko forced us to alter our attacking approach. We responded to his departure by breaking our transfer record again, signing Sébastien Haller from Eintracht Frankfurt for £45m, but he was a very different player to Marko. Seb's game wasn't about running in behind. He needed players running off him and we became much less effective on the counterattack after selling the big Austrian.

Trouble was brewing. We made a decent start to the start of the 2019–20 season and Seb looked settled at first, but we fell apart after losing Łukasz to a serious hip injury at the end of September. It was the beginning of the end for Manuel.

*   *   *

The winter months were hard. Our poor form affected Seb, the crowd started to turn on Manuel and our defensive organisation disappeared, with Roberto deputising for Łukasz in goal.

Roberto's confidence never recovered from making a few mistakes after he came into the team. The situation unsettled our back four and we were going into games knowing that we'd concede at least a couple. Yet Manuel stuck to his guns. He kept picking Roberto, who performed badly when we got smashed by Burnley and Newcastle, and before we knew it we found ourselves fighting against relegation.

It was a swift decline, and Manuel finally acknowledged that we needed to make a change after Spurs turned us over at the London Stadium at the end of November. Our next game was a trip to Chelsea and I was relieved when Manuel told me that he was going to put Dave Martin in goal.

'Okay, boss,' I said. 'I think you need to do it. We need to try someone fresh.'

I felt better after leaving Manuel's office, and I didn't want to keep the news to myself when I spotted Dave in the canteen.

'Make sure you're ready, geez,' I said. 'You're playing on Saturday.'

Dave went silent for a moment. He pondered our fixture list and realised it was Chelsea away. 'No, I'm not,' he said.

'Yes, you are. Make sure you're ready.'

Dave went as white as a ghost. He's a West Ham fan – his dad, Alvin Martin, is fondly remembered as one of the club's best ever centre-backs – and he was over the moon after we signed him during the summer. It was a dream come true for Dave and, although he knew he was coming in to be our third-choice goalkeeper, he didn't take long to click with the lads.

Yet Dave wasn't making any noise when we went to Stamford Bridge. He was always one of the chirpiest ones before a game, but not this time. He simply sat in the corner on his own, refusing to say anything as he prepared for the biggest game of his career.

He needn't have worried. We defended calmly and surprised Chelsea, beating them 1–0 thanks to a slick goal from Cress. Dave couldn't believe it at full-time. The emotion took over as he walked over to the touchline and clambered into the press box to celebrate with his dad. The win meant the world to Dave, and he even saw the funny side when we tried to ruin by moment by claiming he'd actually gone into the stands to hug Moose, TalkSport's infamous reporter.

I was delighted for Dave. Yet we couldn't push on after beating Chelsea. Our problems weren't solely down to the goalkeeping situation. None of us were playing well. I thought that we were going to have a problem holding on to Felipe when pre-season started, but he wasn't the same player any more. His inconsistency frustrated Manuel.

I'm not singling out Felipe, by the way. It was a collective failure. We'd all let ourselves down, and Manuel didn't want to stop playing attacking football. But it was the wrong approach at the time. We were fighting for our lives and needed to dig in. All that mattered was staying up and protecting people's jobs. I wasn't thinking about myself – I always had a sense of pride about the club and the people who worked there, and it hurt when things weren't going well. I worried about the club's finances and I knew that Manuel was feeling the pressure.

I wasn't surprised when the owners told me they were bringing David Moyes back to the club after we lost at home to Leicester at the end of December. We needed to get back to basics. I was happy to oblige when David asked me to come to the stadium for a chat. We sat together for five hours talking about the team, and he listened while I filled him in on the new players and offered my view on what it would take for us to survive.

We were on the same page. David delivered a familiar message when he held a meeting with everyone: you don't run, you don't play. It was time to roll up our sleeves, and I scored twice when we kicked off David's second spell by thrashing Bournemouth 4–0 on New Year's Day.

Yet it still wasn't a happy ship. We proceeded to pick up one point from our next three games, and the atmosphere in the stands was negative when we lost 1–0 at home to West Brom in the fourth round of the FA Cup. I came off the bench and collapsed to the turf after missing a late chance to equalise, although deep down I was relieved not to have earned us a replay. We didn't need an extra game. The situation was grim, even though we brought Tomáš Souček and Jarrod Bowen in before the transfer window shut, and we were in a bad place before hosting Southampton at the end of February.

The fans were grumbling again. Yet the mood in the dressing room was positive. Our performances were improving – we were very unlucky not to beat Liverpool at Anfield – and we weren't worried when the fans staged a protest outside the ground before we played Southampton. The complaints weren't new to us, and we knew from experience not to let dissent from our supporters impact on how we performed.

In any case the fans were with us by the time we kicked off against Southampton. I always had faith in West Ham supporters to back us when we needed them. They know when it's time to put their frustrations to one side, and their positivity played a big part in us ending our long winless run by beating Southampton 3–1.

It was a really good performance. Jarrod gave us loads of energy on the right wing and opened the scoring after fastening on to a clever pass from Pablo Fornals. Everyone knew their jobs. The gaffer had worked hard on tightening up our defence. We weren't as open, we worked on set-pieces and we didn't mind being more direct. Going long played to our strengths. Seb was building a promising partnership with Mic up front and we should have built on our victory over Southampton by beating Arsenal a week later, only to suffer a late defeat after missing countless chances.

But losing to Arsenal didn't affect our morale. Our confidence was back. At that stage the only problem was that the news was full of reports about the emergence of a strange new virus. We all initially thought it was just a mild flu.

*   *   *

The severity of the situation was yet to dawn on us at the start of March 2020. It still seemed like a distant problem and, like the rest of the country, I saw no reason not to go about my daily routine. I trained like normal, before heading into the sauna with Cress and Snods. I didn't take it seriously when they heard my cough and said I must have caught 'this Covid thing'.

But I felt terrible when I got home. I went straight to bed and stayed there for two weeks. My cough was getting worse and my temperature kept going up and down. It wasn't a surprise when the league shut down. Nobody was safe – not even professional athletes. I realised as much when I spoke to the doctor and found out that Cress and Snods were both ill in bed.

I was scared. When I finally mustered the strength to get out of bed I went downstairs to clear out my garage, but I hit a wall after spending four hours down there and had to go back to bed. My back was killing me and I needed to stretch it out. Out of nowhere, though, I felt a burning sensation in my nose.

'Carly, is someone having a fire?' I said, but I couldn't see any smoke when I looked outside. It was bizarre. I didn't think any more of it until Carly served me sausage, mash and onions for dinner. I couldn't taste a thing. I tipped Tabasco sauce all over my plate, but it made no difference.

I felt rough and barely did anything for a month. Meanwhile nobody knew when football was going to come back. We couldn't train and everybody had a lot of spare time on their hands after we went into lockdown. All these trends started up and I decided to give it a go after seeing that people on Instagram were getting nominated to do 5km runs.

I was about 4km in when I thought, 'I'm actually going to die.' I lay down on some grass by the side of the road and found myself struggling to breathe. 'Oh my God,' I thought. 'I didn't realise how much this thing has taken out of me.'

I was absolutely exhausted when I got home. I wasn't unfit, but my lungs wouldn't let me run. To put it into context, I'd managed 4km in 21 minutes. That's probably a decent time for the general public, but it's nowhere for a professional athlete. 'Am I going to be able to recover?' I wondered. 'If the season starts soon, I'm going to be f**ked.'

Little did I know it was going to be a long time before any of us were playing again, nor did I realise that the hardest part of my career was about to begin. Suddenly I was living my life stuck in front of a computer, which wasn't easy for someone with my limited attention span. The kids were at home because the schools were shut and I was constantly on Zoom. It all took an emotional and mental toll. I had my own businesses to look after, and instead of spending time with my family I kept having to attend meetings with the club, the FA, the Premier League and captains from the other 19 sides about the crisis facing football.

It was relentless. I barely slept at night and I'd wake up in the morning thinking, 'I'm going to be on Zoom for another six hours today.' I'm not complaining – plenty of people were in much worse situations than me – but I was so worried about taking care of everyone at West Ham.

I had a lot of conversations with Karren Brady, our Vice-Chairman, and I was over the moon when we agreed that the staff would continue to be paid their full wages and weren't put on furlough. We had to make sure that people could pay their bills and mortgages. I felt responsible again and wanted to make sure that my team-mates were coping. There are a lot of different cultures in our squad and I knew it wouldn't be easy for some of the foreign lads. Pablo Fornals, our Spanish midfielder, had been in England for less than a year and was living on his own in an apartment in Canary Wharf. We had to ensure he didn't feel alone. Even small things like doing our training sessions over Zoom or keeping in touch on WhatsApp helped maintain our team spirit.

As for my position, there were times when I wondered if the pandemic was going to bring my career to a premature end. My contract was up at the end of the season and there was no guarantee that I was going to be given a new one if the league didn't start again soon.

Yet I was more concerned with doing right by other people. I'm so pleased with how the club handled the situation. It meant a lot to me to have the trust of the squad when I negotiated with Karren and the board about deferring our wages, and for them to let me take care of it all. At first the Premier League tried to implement pay cuts across the board because of fears over the TV money drying up, but that was never going to happen. The clubs had to make their own decisions and we weren't opposed to helping non-playing staff by accepting wage deferrals. A good friend helped out with the legal paperwork and the players knew they would get their money back. I had the best personal relationship with Karren and the owners, so the lads knew I was in a good position to make sure everything went smoothly.

I was emotional after we sorted it out. I don't think I could have come back to the club if any staff members had lost their jobs or taken pay cuts. From a moral perspective, there's no way I'd have walked back into the training ground if the kitchen staff and groundsmen I'd known for 20 years had lost money. I wouldn't have wanted to play any part in that. As captain, it was my job to look after people who weren't as fortunate as me. It's why I view the deferrals as one of the biggest achievements of my career. We were West Ham United. The players behaved in the right way, and although the board were facing huge financial challenges, they stepped up to the plate. The owners have taken a lot of stick down the years and have made a few wrong decisions at times, but I'll never forget them doing the right thing when it really mattered.

It was good to see football use the pandemic as a chance to spread positivity. I had a lot of meetings with the other captains and it was inspiring when we came up with the #players together initiative. We played against each other every week and it was an honour to put rivalries to one side while we focused on raising millions for charity.

However, the uncertainty hadn't gone away. Nobody knew the full facts when the discussion turned to playing again. The doctors told us it was unlikely to catch Covid outdoors and that we were young and healthy, so with that in mind it didn't make sense when we were initially told that we had to train alone. There was a lot of confusion and uncertainty, and it was understandable that some players were worried about coming back to play. I was fine, but I wasn't going to judge someone who was living with elderly relatives and didn't want to put their family at risk.

The manager was great. He said he wouldn't force anyone to come to training if they were worried about Covid. Yet the pressure on football to resume was immense. Money talks. We had to give it a go, though a lot of precautions were in place when we went back. At first we went in at staggered times and ran on the pitch on our own, with a fitness coach standing 10 metres away from us. There was none of the usual camaraderie. You got out of your car, walked to the pitch and did your run, then you drove straight back home. It was nice to get out of the house, but it was weird. We couldn't use the treatment room and we were initially told that it wasn't safe to head the ball because there was a danger of getting infected from someone else's sweat.

They were crazy times. While we were adjusting to the new normal at training, the clubs were trying to reach an agreement about what to do if the league was cancelled. Would they declare it null and void? Would they use points-per-game to decide the final standings? Everyone had a different solution, a different agenda. We were just above the bottom three, but we knew there was a chance we'd be sent down by default. The endless debates did my head in. We wanted to play on, but some people wanted to stop. 'What the f**k's going on?' I thought. 'Are we going back? Are we stopping? Do I even need to keep myself fit?'

*　　*　　*

Common sense prevailed in the end. The decision was made for the season to resume and we looked like a solid side when we came back. The lads had kept themselves in good shape and the manager prepared us well.

The one concern was what it would be like to play behind closed doors. Running out into an empty bowl was bizarre when we hosted Wolves in our first game back. We could hear everything the staff were shouting at us from the touchline and the pace was definitely slower. The intensity just wasn't the same without fans roaring us on.

Yet I wasn't worried when we lost 2–0 to Wolves and I didn't panic when Spurs beat us 2–0 three days later. I stayed calm when we were faced with the prospect of losing three consecutive games after we went 1–0 down at home to Chelsea.

I knew we had enough talent. Jarrod and Tomáš were great signings. Mic was flying up front. He bullied Chelsea's defenders and we produced a superb fightback, winning 3–2 after Andriy Yarmolenko cut inside in the last minute and whipped a shot into the bottom corner with his left foot.

Beating Chelsea was a defining moment in our season. Tomáš gave us more power in midfield and I played just in front of him and Dec when four goals from Mic saw us beat Norwich 4–0 at Carrow Road. Mic was on fire. As I said before, he really is one of the most improved players I've ever seen at West Ham and has made himself irreplaceable during the last few years. Centre-backs hated trying to deal with Mic. His physicality was always second to none and he became an even bigger threat after working on improving his technique.

Mic's goals played a huge part in us staying up. We were all but safe after beating Watford 3–1 with two games to go. It was my 500th appearance for West Ham and the manager understood the significance of the moment. 'Look, boys,' David said. 'I'm not going to do my usual team-talk today. You need to win it for Mark. He's been here for 16 years. He's been through all this stuff with Covid on behalf of you boys, so you win tonight and you put yourself safe. Go and win it for him. Not many people achieve 500 appearances for one club.'

I was emotional, needing to hold back the tears, and I was ecstatic after we blew Watford away. It made all those tedious hours spent on Zoom worth it. I was proud to have played 500 times for my boyhood club, and reaching that milestone on the night we secured our Premier League status made the achievement even more special.

I was optimistic about the future. We'd stayed up with relative ease and I expected our progress to continue. We'd benefited from signing some young, hungry, fit players and the lads were buzzing.

'I think we're going to be strong this year,' I said to the manager while we were in Scotland during pre-season. 'I really think we're going to surprise a few people.'

I wasn't getting carried away. There was still a lot of negativity about the club on social media during the summer, but everyone was happy inside the dressing room and we paid no attention to the outside noise. I quickly got over my irritation after we sold Grady Diangana to

West Brom, even though I created a bit of a stink by going on Twitter to question why we'd lost one of our best academy players. With hindsight, I see that such decisions can't be guided by emotion and, ultimately, the club will continue to produce great talents from the academy capable of playing at the highest level.

Opening the 2020–21 season with defeats to Arsenal and Newcastle wasn't a big deal. We were outstanding in our next game, crushing Wolves 4–0 at the London Stadium. Conor Coady, Wolves's captain, was impressed when I spoke to him after the game. 'F**king hell, that was hard work for us,' Conor said. 'You f**king ran us into the ground.'

My confidence was justified. We maintained our momentum when we went to Leicester, who usually gave us a torrid time, and beat them 3–0, and next we went to Spurs and didn't panic after going 3–0 down in the first half. We stuck at it, pulled two goals back and earned a point when Manu scored a stunning goal with the final kick of the game.

It was a massive moment for Manu. He was supposed to be part of Argentina's squad at the 2018 World Cup, only to sustain a serious knee injury on the eve of the tournament. It was hard to watch him go through so much pain. I love Manu like a little brother and it was great to see signs that he was getting back to his best.

I gave Manu a huge cuddle after the game. I was thinking about my wager with my mate Jay, who's a huge Spurs fan. We always played up to the rivalry. This time we said we'd get each other a tailored suit with the result stitched on the inside of the jacket, so I was worried when we were 3–2 down. Jay loves to rub salt in the wound, and I knew he was going to plaster pictures of the suit all over Instagram if Spurs won, so I owed Manu a huge debt of gratitude.

'Manu, thank you so much,' I said. 'I love you, mate. You don't know the pain I'd have gone through if that shot didn't go in.'

That goal was huge for us. I saw the lads celebrating and I knew that our comeback would bring us even closer together. We had such a tight bond. The manager made some shrewd signings, bringing in Saïd Benrahma, Vladimír Coufal and Craig Dawson before the transfer window shut, and we continued to climb the table.

I realised that David was building a team similar to the one he had at Everton. We were strong, talented, quick and athletic. Vlad was a top right-back and a model professional. Pablo and Jarrod gave us creativity in the final third, but we could trust them to focus on the defensive side of the game. The fans loved the hard graft. We were dangerous on the counterattack and we didn't roll over any more. We did things that West Ham weren't known for, like digging deep at Everton on New Year's Day, defending well and winning 1–0 thanks to a late goal from Tomáš.

Tomáš and Vlad were fantastic buys. You never knew what you were going to get from players coming from the Czech league, but our decision to recruit there paid off – Vlad simply wanted to train and play, while Tomáš scored goals, defended the box and put his head where it hurt. The man's got more scars on his face than Rocky. You could always rely on Tomas to turn up. He was fit, he could run and he complemented Dec, who was well on his way to establishing himself as one of the best midfielders around.

I could take losing my place to Dec. At first, though, I found it difficult not to be in the starting 11 every week. It was weird not to know whether my name would be called out when the team was announced on a Friday afternoon. I felt a bit embarrassed as I wasn't used to training while the first team were having a cool down on a Sunday.

But I had to get over it. I put my ego to one side, real-ised that I'd had an incredible career and focused on being a good captain off the pitch. I still had a part to play and I had no intention of joining another club. I wanted to stick it out at West Ham. I had a close relationship with Kevin Nolan, who'd joined the backroom staff, and I made sure that I was ready whenever the manager brought me off the bench to calm things down and help the team close a game out.

I embraced the change. I had a sense that it was coming at the start of the season. I sat with Carly one evening, having a glass of wine with her, and said that I didn't think I was going to play as much any more.

'But maybe that's what you need,' she said. 'You've had 18 years of playing every week. Maybe you need to take a step back.'

Carly knew what I'd gone through during lockdown. She saw my emotions when I was trying to make sure the club didn't suffer from the financial impact of Covid.

'Maybe that's your last big moment of feeling you're responsible for everything,' she said.

Carly was right. I began to enjoy my new role. We were challenging for a place in the Champions League and Dec was going from strength to strength. I realised that my race was almost run. It was time to let everyone know that I was coming to the end.

11

The Perfect Send-Off

first started thinking about retirement during lockdown as I didn't want anyone to tell me that I'd outstayed my welcome at West Ham. I knew it would make everything easier if I was in control and I felt it would help me appreciate my time in the game even more if I could go to bed every night knowing I'd ended my career on my terms.

It was better to leave with everyone wanting more. I thought long and hard about when to call it a day and my mind was made up when I spoke to David Moyes about my plans midway through the 2020–21 campaign. I told him that I wasn't going to stop straight away – I still had another season in me. He knew I was still going to turn up every day, train hard and push the lads to keep their standards high.

There was no chance of me easing off after announcing my retirement. I trained the same way and a lot of people told me that I didn't look like I needed to stop. 'Keep playing,' they said. 'What's wrong with you? You're still one of the top players in training.'

Yet I'd been at West Ham for such a long time. I'd lived and breathed the club since I was 11 years old, so it had reached a point where I needed to make a decision on my future and give myself some clarity.

It made sense to go into my final season knowing it would be my last one. I didn't want the announcement to come out of the blue. I sat down with Dan Francis, our press officer, and asked him to help me write an open letter to the fans. It took us a few drafts to get the wording right, but I was happy with it when we were done. I printed the letter out, took it home and read it to Carly after we'd put the kids to bed. Inevitably, I got emotional and Carly was crying her eyes out when I looked up. West Ham was all we'd ever known. It was strange to think that the end had almost arrived.

However, the story wasn't over yet. The season was going better than anyone could have expected. We were surprise challengers for a place in the top four and I had a part to play when Dec picked up a knee injury a few weeks after I'd gone public with my retirement plans.

Losing Dec was a big blow. He was such a crucial player and I was nervous about deputising for him when we visited Wolves at the start of April. Would my presence stop the team playing well? Would it be my fault if we lost? After all, I wasn't a regular any more. I'd only started one league game since being taken off at half-time during a 2–2 draw with Brighton at the end of December, so it was natural to wonder if I was going to be capable of helping the team cope with Dec's absence.

But the Brighton game was just one of those things. I'd played well in our previous game, even though it was a 3–0 defeat to Chelsea at Stamford Bridge. The manager liked to use me in an advanced role in midfield at times, just in front of Tomáš and Dec, and he decided to give me another start when we played Brighton at home.

It didn't go well, though, and I was taken off at half-time. Part of me wondered if it was because I was the old boy. Everyone was off it before the break and I wasn't having a particularly bad game.

I was upset. I didn't understand David's decision, although I saw where he was coming from when I spoke to him after the game. 'Listen,' he said, 'I just needed to do the right thing for the team. I know we got beat against Chelsea, but you played really well.'

I left it at that. I was past going to the manager's office to bang his door down and ask why I wasn't playing more. 'Right, I'm going to do what's best for the team and just be the same person,' I thought. 'I'm not going to sulk and throw my toys out of the pram.'

There's usually a reward for behaving the right way and staying professional. I stayed patient and played my part when Dec was out. When we beat Wolves at their place in early April, they couldn't handle us during the first half. We'd developed a habit of blowing teams away early on and had become even more of a threat on the counterattack after signing Jesse Lingard on loan from Manchester United during the January transfer window.

Jesse had a big impact on our season. He improved the team and was a bubbly character in the dressing room. We loved him. He kept producing in the final third and he put us on our way at Wolves, opening the scoring with an incredible individual goal.

Wolves couldn't handle us during the first half. We raced into a 3–0 lead and held on when we were under the cosh in the second half. A place in the Champions League was within our grasp. I started again when we beat Leicester 3–2 at home and stayed in the team until I picked up a little calf strain during the dying stages of our 1–0 defeat at home to Chelsea at the end of the month.

Ultimately, we didn't quite have enough depth to finish in the top four. We stumbled in a couple of key games but were still playing for a place in the Europa League when we hosted Southampton on the final day of the season.

It was a wonderful way to end the campaign. We were just starting to come out of lockdown and it was fantastic to see the fans finally allowed back into the London Stadium, even though the attendance was capped at 10,000 because of Covid restrictions. It was a beautiful day. Pablo gave us a 2–0 lead with two nice finishes in the first half and I came off the bench just before Dec charged through in the final minute to seal the 3–0 win that earned us direct qualification into the group stage of the Europa League.

It was like an amazing dream. I saw Carly and the kids waving at me from the stands, and I was buzzing when I went away on holiday. No one had tipped us to finish sixth, and the thought of playing in Europe during my final season in claret and blue filled me with excitement. I couldn't wait to get going. I knew it was going to be special.

* * *

I was confident that we could have a proper go at the Europa League. We had a nice balance of everything in the squad. We were strong, talented and athletic, and the only thing I was worried about while I was on holiday was heading back for pre-season at the age of 34 and trying to keep up with all the young pups.

The manager had brought in so many fit and hungry young players, and I was looking forward to seeing Dec push on again. I was so proud of his performances for England during that summer. He was incredibly influential when they reached the final of Euro 2020, and me and Lenny were lucky enough to get the chance to head over to Wembley for a couple of England's games.

It was the first time I'd ever gone to watch a match with my boy. James Corden gave us tickets in his box and we were over the moon when we attended England's victory over Germany in the last 16 of the Euros. Dec had an amazing game and I was delighted for him. I spoke to him three times a day during the Euros and texted him the same line before every game: 'Be Declan Rice'.

I knew Dec wouldn't have any problems if he stayed true to himself. I backed him to stand tall when England played Italy in the final. I was at the game with Lenny and we both had so much faith in him. I was baffled when England took him off during the final. Obviously Gareth Southgate knows more about management than I do, but nobody can tell me that Dec wasn't England's best player by a mile. The Italy midfielders simply couldn't live with him. He was too quick and strong; he kept surging past them, kept driving England up the pitch. So I was staggered when I saw his number go up during the second half.

I kept coming back to that decision after Italy won on penalties. It was gut-wrenching. Lenny was devastated. He really thought football was coming home, and England winning meant even more to him because he has such a tight bond with Dec. There are times when I go into Lenny's room and find him on FaceTime with Dec, just chatting away about football. It's lovely to see.

But Lenny was too young to understand that an England win wasn't guaranteed. He was jumping up and down when it went to penalties, but I simply sat there, worrying for the lads who were going to take one. I felt for Marcus Rashford, Jadon Sancho and Bukayo Saka when they missed their penalties. It's a horrible feeling, as I know all too well, and it was hard to watch Lenny crying his eyes out while we were driving home.

I was gutted too. I almost went home when Dec went off. I couldn't work it out. The only explanation is that his body language sometimes fools people into thinking that he's tired. He's got an incredible engine, and I've told him that he has to do a better job of hiding it when he feels knackered.

This is a kid who could play a game every day if necessary. People underestimated his fitness when we visited Newcastle on the opening day of the 2021–22 season. A lot was made of Allan Saint-Maximin beating Dec on the right flank before crossing for Callum Wilson to put

Newcastle 1–0 up after five minutes. Pundits thought it was because Dec was tired after the Euros, but the truth is that Saint-Maximin could have done that to anyone. All that stuff about a short pre-season was irrelevant. Obviously we hammered Dec after the game, telling him that Saint-Maximin had sent him off to fetch a Mars Bar from the stands, but he raised his level in the second half, driving us on as we fought back to win 4–2.

We looked good. We invested in the squad, bolstering our defence by buying Kurt Zouma from Chelsea and giving ourselves another option in attack with the signing of Nikola Vlašić, and we impressed again when we smashed Leicester 4–1 in our second game.

Leicester couldn't live with the quality of our football. It was an emotional occasion, the first time we'd played in front of a full crowd at home for almost two years, and the atmosphere was something else when Saïd Benrahma put us 2–0 up at the start of the second half. I was on the bench, sitting next to Dave Martin, and he had goose-bumps on his arm when Said scored. It was already gearing up to be another memorable season.

*　　*　　*

It was a great time to be a West Ham player. Everything was flowing on the pitch and our team spirit was unrivalled during my final few years as a professional. People like Couf and Big Tom were ready to run through brick walls for the club and I had so much love for Pablo Fornals. He took time to adapt to English football after joining us from Villarreal in 2019, but he never gave up. Pablo was determined to make it work at West Ham. He knuckled down, played in loads of positions for the team and tried hard even when he wasn't having the best of games.

Players with that kind of attitude are invaluable. Pablo knew that being technically gifted wasn't enough in the Premier League. His enthusiasm was infectious, he demanded so much from himself, and while he got emotional with himself at times, his work ethic was an example for others to follow.

The culture at the club had changed. Jarrod Bowen, who was a quiet lad and a superb professional, didn't think that his goals and assists meant that he didn't have to track back. We were an honest bunch and we all bounced off each other in the dressing room. Nobody caused any trouble. I'd heard some worrying stories about Saïd before he joined us from Brentford in October 2020, but he proved me wrong. He delivered goals and assists for the team, has a really good sense of humour and clicked with the other

French speakers in the squad, Issa, Kurt, Alphonse Areola and Arthur Masuaku.

We had a wonderful mixture of characters and there was so much laughter in the dressing room. It was carnage at times, and because we trained so hard nobody had any complaints about how much we messed around off the pitch.

There were so many ridiculous pranks. Big Daws was a funny bastard, people like Dec and Ryan Fredericks were always involved, and I had a reputation as one of the worst offenders, though I was on the receiving end when I agreed to do 500 metres as quickly as possible on the rowing machine on my 34th birthday. The music was pumping in the gym, and I wasn't prepared for it when the boys ran in and chucked egg and flour all over me.

Nothing was off limits. You can say anything to me and I won't take offence. I gave as good as I got and had a long running battle with Snods. I haven't forgotten what he did to my Ugg slippers. I'd just bought the new iPhone and was in the changing room at the training ground one morning, chatting to Cress, when I saw a chance to wind up Snods.

'F**king hell, Snods, look at your old iPhone,' I said. 'What's the matter with you, you tight bastard?'

But there was no reaction from him. He was usually up for a laugh, but he wasn't biting this time. I turned back to

Cress and picked up one of my slippers, only to realise that Snods had done me over. There was a huge piece of shit in my slipper and when I turned around Snods was rolling around on the floor, killing himself with laughter.

The back and forth between us was relentless. There was almost a serious incident after I messed up one of Snods's credit cards. He responded by hiding my wallet and refused to give it back. 'Snods, I need my wallet,' I said. 'You can't just take the whole thing.'

'I don't give a f**k,' he said. 'It's gone.'

I had to hit back. I waited a day before going to the player care team. They had my wallet and I told them not to tell Snods that they'd given it to me. I had a plan. I wanted him to think that it was still missing. I saw him laughing with Cress and decided to have another go. 'Snods, I need my wallet,' I said. 'This is taking the piss now.'

'I ain't got it.'

Everything was coming together perfectly. I always take my two huge dogs to the training ground, so I went off to the car park during the afternoon and took them out of the van out while the lads were having a coffee. 'Mate,' I said when Snods came bolting over to get into his car, 'you ain't getting home until you give me my wallet back.'

I was deadly serious. The dogs were by my side and I wasn't messing around. Snods tried to make a move, but he sprinted back into the building as soon as I made my dogs bark at him.

I was pissing myself. I had the wallet and Snods was completely oblivious. All of a sudden, though, I saw a side door open. There's a big hedge near the car park and I could see Snods trying to creep past us. Unfortunately, though, so did my big male dog. Strikes didn't wait. He just charged. 'Holy f**k!' I thought. 'He's going to bite him!'

Snods immediately turned and ran. Pieces of the bush went flying in the air and I managed to stop Strikes just in the nick of time.

It was a lucky escape. However, I didn't stop laying into Snods. He was on the verge of joining West Brom and he turned up five minutes late for a team meeting ahead of our trip to Everton at the start of 2021. He was shaking his head, trying to make out it wasn't his fault, but I couldn't wait to get stuck into him.

'Snods, listen,' I said when the meeting was over. 'I know you're leaving, mate, but you're not taking this seriously. You can't be late for meetings.'

'Oh, f**k off,' he said. 'I've got an issue to take care of. Something's going on.'

'I don't care, mate,' I said. 'You can't be late.'

I wasn't going to let it go. Me and Cress peppered Snods all the way up to Everton. Then, when we were having dinner on the night before the game, a member of the player care team sent a message to our group chat, letting us know that there was a team meeting at 8 p.m.

There was just one catch: only the starting 11 were meant to be there. Me and Snods were both on the bench, but I knew he hadn't read the message properly. 'Just go with it,' I said to the lads. 'Oi, Snods. Don't be late to this meeting at 8. You've already been late once today.'

Nobody said a word. I jumped up at 7.55 p.m. and headed towards the lift with seven players who were starting against Everton. Snods still wasn't paying attention. He came along with us and when the lift opened I turned around, pretending that I'd left my room key on the table and telling the others to head upstairs without me.

Snods didn't suspect a thing. He bowled into the meeting room and sat in the front row. The gaffer's assistants – Paul Nevin, Kev Nolan and Stuart Pearce – were bemused. 'F**king hell,' Snods went. 'Nobes is late, isn't he?'

But nobody said a word. Cress was dying with laughter. Slowly, it dawned on him. 'You're not playing tomorrow, Snods,' Pearcey said. 'You need to get out.'

It was perfection. I was in my room and I had tears rolling down my cheek when Snods knocked on the door. The humiliation was written all over his face. 'I've never been so embarrassed in all my life,' he said.

* * *

The pranks probably sound immature to outsiders, but it's important to blow off some steam with your team-mates. The banter in the dressing room is what I miss more than anything else. I loved that side of the game – the camaraderie, the piss-taking, the simplicity of going in every day and knowing that something funny's going to happen. There has to be a balance between work and play. We were bang on in training and having a laugh off the pitch brought us closer together.

It was a pleasure to work in that environment. Everyone bounced off each other and I'm so grateful that the lads succeeded in making sure my final season was packed with special memories.

Playing in Europe was beautiful. I was excited when we flew to Croatia to play Dinamo Zagreb in our first group game. Our form was excellent, and while we didn't have much European experience, we didn't want to make any changes to our approach. We analysed Dinamo closely, picked out areas where we could beat them and proved to be far too strong for them on the night.

I found the experience slightly disappointing. Dinamo didn't offer much, their fans didn't create a particularly intimidating atmosphere and we cruised to a comfortable 2–0 win thanks to goals from Mic and Dec.

Still, I was glad to get on for the final 20 minutes. We were off the mark and all my mates were in the away end.

I was pleased we'd finally given our fans a chance to have a proper European tour. The adventure was under way and we wanted to make the most of it.

They were great times. We flew straight back to London after the game, spent the night in a hotel in Stratford and treated ourselves by ordering a takeaway. There was a big group of us – me, Dec, Cress, Freddo, Dave Martin, Angelo and Ben Johnson – and it ended up becoming our routine whenever we won in Europe.

Of course, it wasn't plain sailing all the way. We hosted United three days after beating Dinamo, and all eyes were on me when we won a penalty in the final minute of stoppage time.

I didn't hesitate when the manager asked me to come off the bench and make it 2–2 with the final kick of the game. I don't subscribe to the view that you should never bring someone on to take a penalty. I was fine physically. The manager had spent the entire second half telling me to warm up and I was ready when he brought me on for Jarrod.

It simply wasn't meant to be. David de Gea went the right way, made a top save and earned United the three points. I felt absolutely sick. It was like I'd let everyone down, and to make matters worse Jesse Lingard, who scored United's last-minute winner, came into our dressing room to take the piss out of me after the game.

The lads were just as ruthless as Jesse. They barely waited 10 minutes before they started hammering me, telling me that I only came on because I wanted to be the hero and save the day. I suppose you've got to laugh. There are more important things in life than a penalty and, looking at it rationally, I was only trying to earn us a draw in a league game.

I would have been more annoyed with myself if I'd told the manager not to put me on. I would have gone to bed every night kicking myself for chickening out. At least I knew the outcome after De Gea came out on top against me.

At the time, though, I was mentally scarred. I had a horrible feeling when I thought about taking my next penalty. I started when we played Manchester City in the fourth round of the League Cup and I felt the anxiety rising when I looked up at the clock with 20 minutes left. 'It's still 0–0,' I thought. 'There's no extra-time. This is going to penalties. F**k's sake – I can't go through that pain again.'

This time, though, I left nothing to chance when I stepped up in the shootout. Carly had begged me not to take any more penalties after my miss against United, but that was never going to happen – I had to step up. I'd made up my mind after about 80 minutes against City: aim high and send it straight down the middle. I didn't want to go through my usual routine of waiting for the keeper to make a move. I knew they rarely stand still and it was such a relief when the ball hit the back of the net.

The night belonged to us. Phil Foden missed for City and we were through to the quarter-finals when Saïd stuck his spot-kick away. It was another fantastic achievement. We were going places and the stadium finally felt like home. The stands behind the goal looked better after being squared off and surrounding the pitch with a claret carpet made a difference. Everything started to flow. The staff knew the players, the lounges were better and Hugo Scheckter made a lot of improvements while he was the club's head of player care.

The player liaison team are really important. Stuart Brown has done a great job since replacing Hugo, and the squad had a lot of respect for George Stannard and Charley Harding.

The club had pieced itself back together. The fans felt a connection with the team and I was emotional when we hosted Rapid Vienna in our second group game. Everyone was talking about it. Me and Dec were asked to attend when the statue of Bobby Moore, Sir Geoff Hurst and Martin Peters was unveiled on the day before the game, and I was delighted when the manager told me that I was going to start against Vienna. 'I need your experience,' he said. 'I'm going to play you tomorrow night.'

It was an honour to think that I was going to lead the team out in Europe. Everything felt so positive. I sat next to Dec before the game and I told him that he had to get forward. 'You've got me in there tonight, so you push on,' I said. 'Get in the box.'

I knew that Dec was more than a holding midfielder. He's so powerful and it was a great moment when he burst into the box to give us the lead after 29 minutes. It's not often that something like that happens after you've talked about it in the dressing room. It's why we were both so happy when Dec scored.

It was another experience to savour. Saïd made it 2–0 with a nicely taken goal and we were on the verge of reaching the last 16 after beating Genk 3–0 at home at the end of October.

We'd adapted to European football. Meanwhile we were continuing to challenge in the league, deservedly beating Chelsea, Liverpool and Spurs at home before Christmas. No wonder the fans came up with the 'West Ham are massive' chant. I genuinely thought that we were going to win when we played Liverpool at the start of November. They were a great side, but I didn't fear anyone. 'This must be how the big teams feel,' I thought. 'It's beautiful.'

*   *   *

We were third after beating Liverpool 3–2. At that stage I really thought we were going to qualify for the Champions League. The only problem, though, was that we still had a small squad. The workload was massive, and it started to catch up with us when we lost a few influential defenders to injury just before Christmas.

We simply weren't used to playing so much football. We weren't at full strength when we lost to Spurs in the last eight of the League Cup, and it reached a point where the manager decided that he had to put a bigger emphasis on the Europa League.

We knew that we had a chance of going all the way after finishing top of our group. All anyone could think about was playing Sevilla in the last 16. They have a great record in the competition, but we weren't scared of them. The mood was positive when we flew to Spain for the first leg. The sun was shining, the atmosphere at the Rámon Sánchez-Pijuán Stadium was amazing, the pitch was beautiful and I was buzzing when the manager brought me off the bench with seven minutes remaining.

There was no reason for us to be downbeat after Sevilla secured a narrow 1–0 win. We created plenty of chances and had a good look at them. They were far from unbeatable. We knew that we could hurt them and it was a massive advantage to have the second leg at our place.

Everyone was up for it when Sevilla came to the London Stadium. The noise from the crowd was deafening and we backed ourselves to score against anyone at home – we simply had to keep it tight at the back. Our belief grew after Alphonse kept us in it early on, making a vital save to stop Sevilla scoring the opening goal on the night.

It was a huge moment. We pushed on after Alphonse's heroics and levelled the tie on aggregate when Big Tom headed in a cross from Mic just before half-time. The plan was coming together. We were the better side and had chances to win it in normal time.

Yet we couldn't quite find the crucial second goal before the 90 minutes were up. The tension grew during extra-time. I was on the bench, and the longer we went without making the breakthrough the more I started to panic about the manager asking me to come on if the game went to a penalty shootout. 'Please,' I thought. 'Not penalties.'

My mind inevitably went back to my miss against United. Yet I didn't have to worry. The ending was written in the stars as soon as Andriy Yarmolenko came off the bench. He'd been through a horrendous time after Russia's invasion of Ukraine. He'd always been calm about the situation in the past, telling me that Russia were always making threats, and I felt sick for him when the war started. He was so scared for his family, who were still in the country, and I wouldn't have blamed him if he'd decided to stop playing football.

But that wasn't Yarma. He took some time off, somehow managed to get his family to the UK and made a dramatic return when he came on against Aston Villa at the London Stadium, opening the scoring with a really clever goal.

Yarma was at it again when we hosted Sevilla four days after our 2–1 win over Villa. It had to be him who was waiting to convert the rebound after Bono, Sevilla's goalkeeper, pushed out a shot from Pablo. Yarma's such a great guy, and I'll always be grateful to him for showing the courage to come back and score one of the most important goals in West Ham's entire history.

It was an extraordinary moment. We'd knocked out the favourites and weren't fazed when we landed Lyon in the last eight. They had a lot of talented players, but they were 10th in Ligue 1 and the scouting report from Issa and Arthur was encouraging. They told us that Lyon played good football but had a lot of players who didn't like tracking back, which was obviously going to cause them problems when they came up against our quality on the counterattack.

Lyon didn't make life easy for us when they came to London for the first leg, however. We were up against it after Cress was shown a red card for fouling Moussa Dembélé on the stroke of half-time. We held out with 10 men, even taking a shock lead when Jarrod scored at the start of the second half, but Lyon thought that the tie was theirs to lose after they pulled it back to 1–1.

We weren't impressed with their cockiness. We took note of Dembélé's wink after Cress's sending off. We saw their social media team tweet that there was no chance of them failing to go through. It fired us up. We had a point to prove when we crossed the Channel for the second leg. We knew that Mic's pace would hurt them on the counter-attack, and although we rode our luck during the first 20 minutes, we stayed calm, kept our composure and waited for an opportunity to strike.

The difference is that we were more of a team than Lyon. They were bad at defending set-pieces and we went ahead when Daws shouldered in a corner from Pablo just before half-time. It was a great time to score. Lyon completely lost their discipline and we quickly doubled our lead when Dec scored from the edge of the area.

I was so proud of the lads. We were pinching ourselves when Jarrod raced through to make it 3–0 at the start of the second half and, having spent ages telling Kev Nolan to get the manager to put me on, I was over the moon when I was given the chance to come off the bench during the dying stages.

It was one of my favourite games in a West Ham shirt. It didn't matter that I'd only played the final 13 minutes.

It was special to be involved and I couldn't believe that we were through to a European semi-final.

The celebrations were amazing. I cried when I spoke to Carly and the kids on FaceTime. We went back out to thank our travelling fans, who weren't allowed to leave the ground until long after the final whistle. I even made headlines after Rob Pritchard, who works in the media department, took a photo of me sweeping up the away dressing room.

Social media went wild when that picture appeared on the club's Twitter account. It wasn't a big deal, though. I always made sure to tidy up after an away game. I'd committed to doing it ever since I came back into the dressing room after a game at Sheffield United and found that we'd left it in an absolute state. I felt embarrassed for the club and promised that it would never happen again.

It costs nothing to show respect to staff members who work behind the scenes at clubs up and down the country. Sometimes new players would ask me why I was sweeping up, but I simply told them that there was no excuse for everyone else not to get involved if they saw me doing it.

It's important to keep standards high. There was a lot of talk before the second leg against Lyon about Issa playing instead of Kurt, who was out with an ankle injury, but we defended brilliantly. It goes to show that you need to keep every member of your squad happy. Issa stepped up when we needed him and Daws, who came into the side after we lost Angelo to a serious knee injury, was also going from strength to strength in central defence.

The fans loved Daws. They celebrated like it was a goal when he crashed into three challenges in a row during the first leg against Lyon. He became a cult figure with the supporters and we were amused when they started calling him Ballon Dawson. 'Daws,' Ben Johnson said, 'I think you actually will be nominated for it this year.'

* * *

Anything seemed possible after we made it past Lyon. We knew we'd become West Ham legends if we could make it to Seville for the final and lift the trophy. It felt so close, although I was gutted not to be playing Barcelona in the last four. We fully expected to be going to the Nou Camp after learning that our semi-final opponents would either be Barca or Eintracht Frankfurt. It would have been such a glamorous tie, especially in my final season, and everyone was surprised when we heard that Eintracht had gone through.

I was concerned. Barca going out lulled people into a false sense of security, but I wasn't going to make the mistake of taking Eintracht lightly. 'You've got to be good to beat Barca over two legs,' I said. 'They play a tricky formation and they're a dangerous side.'

My fears were well founded. The first leg was at our place and Eintracht killed us by scoring inside the first minute. It was like they'd stuck a pin in the balloon and let the air out. The goal completely knocked us off our stride and nothing really went for us on the night. We were unlucky to hit the woodwork three times, and although Mic hauled us level before the break, we had it all to do after falling to a 2–1 defeat.

It was an uphill battle. Eintracht weren't the best team we'd faced in the competition, but they set themselves up well and we weren't quite at it. It was frustrating. We believed that we could turn it around when we went to Germany for the second leg, but it wasn't our night. Eintracht seemed to have all the momentum and their fans were astonishing. I've never experienced such a well-orchestrated atmosphere. I marvelled at the flares, the banners and the lighting. Everyone was singing and I couldn't take my eyes off their fans during the first 20 minutes.

It was a phenomenal sight. My mates who were in the West Ham section of the crowd said they were drowned out by whistles every time they tried to make themselves heard. It was like we were extras in Eintracht's show, and everything that could go wrong did go wrong. We made a decent start, but it all unravelled when Cress was sent off in the first half. It wasn't long before we were 1–0 down. It was hard to see a way back, even though we played pretty well with 10 men. Dec was like two players in midfield, but even he couldn't save us.

I felt sick when it was over. Everyone was emotional and angry. Ben Johnson was crying his eyes out and I was absolutely gutted for Cress. He was my team-mate for eight years and we're really close. I sat next to him in the dressing room and left it five minutes before trying to cheer him up. 'At what point do I f**king hammer you for f**king this up?' I said.

It wasn't Cress's fault that we lost. Eintracht deserved to go through and were worthy winners of the tournament. There was nothing we could do about it. Looking on the bright side, I felt blessed to have gone on such an incredible journey. It would have been brilliant to have given the fans another day out and I'll probably never get over the pain of losing that semi-final. I'll probably always close my eyes at night and think 'What if?' But at the same time I'll also smile about the memories we made and the fact I got to enjoy our run with a special group of players.

We had to get on with it. We still had a chance of qualifying for Europe via our league position, and I knew that my time was coming to an end. I couldn't escape it. Every time I had treatment from Craig, our masseur, he'd say something like, 'This is the last time we're ever going to do this at Man United away.' It went on all season and it was bizarre when I left training before our game against Brighton on the final day of the season. 'F**king hell,' I thought. 'I need to clear my locker out.'

There were so many people I was going to miss. I gave the kitchen staff a cuddle. I thought about how strange it was going to be not to give Anita in the front office a kiss on the cheek every morning. Even taking my boots away for the final time made my bottom lip wobble.

But it was time to say goodbye. I thought about Dad. I always looked forward to him sending me a congratulatory message if I'd played well, but even he was drained by the end. He was relieved when I was slowly being eased out of the team. I understand the pressure. Now I have time to watch Honey play netball and I can't focus on anyone other than Lenny when he's playing football. I'm way more invested in their achievements. Carly's even had to stop me running on the pitch to celebrate when Lenny made a catch during a cricket match at school.

It's nice to take a step back and spend more time with my family. I was mentally exhausted by the time I came on during the dying stages of our 3–1 defeat to Brighton, whose second-half comeback forced us to settle for a place in the Europa Conference League. To be honest I'd more or less checked out after facing Manchester City in my final home game a week earlier. It was such an intense period. Everyone wanted a piece of me and I needed to make time for all the people who'd helped me out down the years.

I didn't mind constantly being asked if I had a spare five minutes. I knew that everyone only wanted to make my farewell as memorable as possible. There was a lovely presentation at the training ground and the staff all chipped in with a bit money to buy me a few bits and pieces.

It was heartfelt. I'm incredibly blessed to have been born in east London, play for West Ham and captain the club. It was a huge honour and I could never have dreamt of the send-off I was given after the City game.

I didn't know much about what the club were planning. They put so much thought into it and the organisation was outstanding, but my main focus was on making sure we were ready to take on City when I sat down with the manager during the week.

'Look, boss, the first priority is getting a result,' I said. 'We need the points for Europe, so don't make this about me. It's going to be about me afterwards, so put your strongest team on the pitch. If you need me, you need me. If you don't, you don't. That's it. Don't feel you somehow have to involve me just because I played for West Ham for 18 years.'

Of course, it was beautiful to get on during the second half. It was a great game. We were superb in the first half, taking a 2–0 lead thanks to two fine goals from Jarrod, but City refused to lie down. They fought back to 2–2 after the break and I made sure to give Łukasz a big hug after he earned us a point by saving a late penalty from Riyad Mahrez.

It would have been a shame if we'd lost that game. As it was, everyone was happy. City were a step closer to winning the title and it meant a lot to me when their manager Pep Guardiola bowed and shared a few private words with me after the game.

I was touched by how much people cared. I went back to the dressing room, and it was amazing to see that the ground was still full when I came back out for the post-match ceremony. Nobody wanted to go home. The fans knew I was one of them and the club pulled out all the stops. They put on food and drinks for my family and friends after the game, and the celebrations went on for a long time, until eventually me and Carly were the only ones left.

We were blown away. I was an emotional wreck. I went into London to spend the night with Carly, and I cried my eyes out when she gave me a watch as a gift. In the end it was all about family. I knew I couldn't go to bed without giving Dad a call.

'I've never seen anything like it,' he said. 'I've been a West Ham fan all my life. I've been a football fan all my life. I've never seen love like that. You should feel incredibly privileged and thankful for that send-off. West Ham have given you so much. It was truly special.'

Picture Credits

Page 7 (middle): RvS.Media/Basile Barbey/Getty Images
Page 7 (bottom): Glyn Kirk/AFP via Getty Images
Page 8 (top): Jacques Feeney/Offside
Page 8 (bottom): PA Images/Alamy Stock Photo